£12.52

9

00017575

ARTHUR MILLER

A View from the Bridge

Introduction and questions by
Tim Bezant

Heinemann Educational,
a division of Heinemann Publishers (Oxford) Ltd
Halley Court, Jordan Hill, Oxford OX2 8EJ
OXFORD LONDON EDINBURGH
MADRID ATHENS BOLOGNA PARIS
MELBOURNE SYDNEY AUCKLAND SINGAPORE TOKYO
IBADAN NAIROBI HARARE GABORONE PORTSMOUTH NH (USA)

First published in the *Hereford Plays* series by Heinemann Educational 1975
First published in the *Heinemann Plays* series 1995

10 9 8 7 6 5 4 3 2 1
99 98 97 96 95

A catalogue record for this book is available from the British Library on request.
ISBN 0 435 23312 2

All applications for a licence to perform this play must be made in advance to the author's agent, Elaine Greene Ltd, 31 Newington Green, London N16 9PU. No performance may take place unless a licence has been obtained.

Cover design by Keith Pointing

Original design by Jeffery White Creative Associates

Typeset by TechType, Abingdon, Oxon

Printed by Clays Ltd, St Ives plc

CONTENTS

PREFACE

In this edition of *A View from the Bridge*, you will find notes, questions and activities to help in studying the play in class, particularly at GCSE level.

The introduction provides background information on the author and on the social context of the play. It outlines the story, discusses performance and examines the characters in detail.

The activities at the end of the book range from straightforward *Keeping Track* questions which can be tackled at the end of each act to focus close attention on what is happening in the play, to more detailed work on character, performance, themes and criticism in the *Explorations* section.

There is also a bibliography detailing other works by Miller, as well as critical studies.

If you are already using the Hereford edition of *A View from the Bridge*, you will find that the page numbering in the actual playscript is the same, allowing the two editions to be easily used side by side.

INTRODUCTION

Arthur Miller

Arthur Miller was born on October 17th, 1915, in New York City. His parents were both immigrants into the United States. The family lived in prosperity due to the success of his father's clothing manufacturing business, but this collapsed, along with the American economy as a whole, following the Wall Street Crash. As a result, Miller had to work as a warehouseman in order to save his fees before he was able to go to Michigan University in 1934 to study Economics and History.

While at university Miller also followed a course in playwriting and this now became his primary ambition. After graduating in 1938, he earned his living from journalism and from writing radio scripts. During World War Two he also worked as a shipfitter for two years in the Brooklyn Navy Shipyard, where a 'near majority of the workers were Italian' and where Miller 'made connections with their family-centred concerns … [which were] full of Sicilian dramas' (*Timebends*). His first professionally produced stage play, *The Man Who Had All the Luck*, was a failure when it was staged on Broadway in 1944, but in 1947 *All My Sons* was a considerable success. This was followed in 1949 by *Death of a Salesman*, which was awarded the Pulitzer Prize, and in 1953 by *The Crucible,* which Miller wrote as a reaction to the witch-hunt of left-wing sympathizers which was current in the United States. Miller himself was summoned as a left-wing sympathizer before the House of Representatives UnAmerican Activities Committee, which had been set up to investigate people who it believed were acting against the interests of the United States. Although Miller was fined for non-co-operation with the Committee, his sentence was later quashed.

A View from the Bridge was Miller's next play. It was first produced as a one-act play in verse in 1955: the revised and extended two-act play followed in 1956 when it was presented at the Comedy Theatre in London. In the same year Miller divorced his first wife and married the actress and star Marilyn Monroe, although this marriage was also to end in divorce in 1961. Miller continued to write, producing plays including *After the Fall* (1964), which many critics interpreted as a reflection upon his relationship with Monroe, *The Price* (1968), *The Archbishop's Ceiling* (1977), *The American Clock* (1980) and *Broken Glass* (1994). In addition, Miller's autobiography, *Timebends*, was published in 1987.

In a career that has spanned more than half a century, Miller has become America's and one of the world's most important and influential playwrights. Many of his plays examine the position of the individual in relation to their responsibilities and position in society and may be seen, as a result, to be political. At all times, however, they reveal a deep and sympathetic understanding of how people think, behave and react to the world around them, in particular when they find themselves in situations which threaten to overwhelm and defeat them. It is this ability to dramatize the attempts to find the necessary balance between the conflicting demands of private and public life that is Miller's hallmark as a writer.

A View from the Bridge

A View from the Bridge has its roots in the late 1940s when Miller became interested in the work and lives of the communities of dockworkers and longshoremen of New York's Brooklyn harbour and where he had himself previously worked. To Miller, this was 'a dangerous and mysterious world at the water's edge that drama and literature had never touched' (*Timebends*). Miller found that the 'waterfront was the Wild West, a desert beyond the law', populated and worked by people who were poorly paid, exploited by their bosses and who were in many cases only recent immigrants to the United States, having come to America, as Miller's parents had done, in hope of the work, wealth and security that their home countries could not guarantee.

It was during this time that a young lawyer friend of Miller's 'mentioned a story he'd recently heard of a longshoreman who had ratted to the Immigration Bureau on two brothers, his own relatives, who were living illegally in his very home, in order to break an engagement between one of them and his niece' (*Timebends*). Miller noted the story but, being preoccupied with other projects, did not act upon it immediately.

A few years later, during his first visit to Italy, Miller visited Sicily, where he 'saw a dozen men standing around a well in the middle of a dusty piazza'. There he learnt that it was the habit of these men to gather there in the vain hope that a local estate might need an extra worker. 'Always hungry, they were offering themselves, but all they were eating was time' (*Timebends*). This image attached itself to the story Miller had heard earlier and, combined with the experiences he had gained of Italian immigrant workers in the Brooklyn Navy Yard, provided the background to the play that was to become *A View from the Bridge*.

The first version of the play was in one act, written in verse: Miller intended the play to be a modern version of a Greek tragedy (in which a central character is led by fate towards a destiny that cannot be escaped). In the full-length version of the play Miller retained much of the content of the verse but transformed it into prose. Since its original production in 1956, it has been performed worldwide, the most successful recent production being at London's National Theatre in 1987.

In Performance

In the opening stage directions Miller sets the play, very precisely, in Red Hook, 'the slum that faces the bay on the seaward side of Brooklyn Bridge ... the gullet of New York'. The Carbones' living and dining room is the focus of the action, but the street outside must also be partly represented so that the audience is immediately made aware of both the private and the public contexts in which the action is set: quite literally, we see Eddie and Beatrice's place in the community. While a high degree of realism is appropriate in the design of the Carbone family home, the street itself need only be suggested.

The precision of the setting is also reflected in the language of the play. While Alfieri, the first character whom the audience meets, speaks a recognizable standard American English, the Carbones (and their cousins) speak in conversational Brooklynese, the patterns and rhythms of which reveal the lack of formal education and the deprivation experienced by the characters ('Listen, I could tell you things about Louis which you wouldn't wave to him no more'). This is a language which is direct, vigorous and expressive both of what the characters mean and of what they are unable to communicate directly. This may be, of course, because they lack the language to express themselves fully or because they do not wish to put their ideas into words (as is frequently the case between Eddie, Beatrice and Catherine).

By the end of Alfieri's first speech, the audience knows that the events they are watching will be 'bloody' in their conclusion. They share Alfieri's perspective, looking back on the events which he narrates. This perspective in turn heightens their sympathies for the other characters of the play as their story is told in what is in effect a series of flashbacks; it further serves to heighten the sense of tragedy that develops as the play progresses. For despite Alfieri's best efforts, the events that follow are inevitable and reminiscent of the characters' homeland, Italy.

It is Eddie Carbone who is identified by Alfieri as the hero of this particular tragedy. Eddie is fundamentally a simple, straightforward man who 'worked on the piers when there was work, he brought home his pay, and he lived'; he is seen to be humorous, kind and generous in anticipating the arrival, illegally, of his wife Beatrice's cousins. He is also, however, over-protective of his orphaned niece, Catherine, in her increasing maturity. It is this urge to protect Catherine, to keep her from discovering her independence, that makes him increasingly sensitive to the presence of Beatrice's cousins and to Rodolfo in particular, to whom Catherine rapidly becomes attracted.

Eddie's wife, Beatrice, is aware of a deeper, more disturbing reason for Eddie's protectiveness towards Catherine. It soon becomes clear that she is unhappy about Eddie's attitude to his niece and, initially, she is able to persuade him to allow Catherine to start work when the opportunity arises. But the problems between Eddie and Beatrice go deeper: Beatrice has 'other worries' about when she is 'gonna be a wife again'. The physical, sexual part of the Carbones' marriage has broken down and, despite challenging Eddie over this, Beatrice is unable to make him face why this might be, let alone make him admit his weakness to himself, and she remains powerless as a result.

For it is Marco and Rodolfo's arrival at the Carbones' that is the catalyst for Catherine finally achieving adulthood. Previously she has been supported by the Carbones as she has worked her way through school, doting on Eddie, and has been, in effect, their surrogate daughter. But her finding work and her growing attraction to Rodolfo, which leads to their planned marriage, brings out an increasingly aggressive reaction in Eddie that starts to break the family apart. Catherine becomes more rebellious and independent and Beatrice becomes increasingly frustrated as she realizes how events will go. For Beatrice has realized what she says to Eddie only as the climax of the tragedy approaches, that he wants 'somethin' else, Eddie, and you can never have her!'

Eddie's obsession with Catherine is something he is not able to recognize or understand for himself. Instead, he focuses his anger and frustration upon Rodolfo, the younger of Beatrice's cousins. While Marco is a stronger, more reticent man who has come to America to earn money he can then send home to his starving wife and children in Italy, and who quickly earns a reputation for hard work, Rodolfo has no such responsibilities and has a more frivolous, light-hearted attitude to life. It is this that Catherine finds attractive and Eddie finds repulsive and unmanly. Eddie is also suspicious of Rodolfo's interest in Catherine, believing that he seeks to marry her in order to gain American citizenship. It becomes clear to both Catherine and to the audience that, for all his youthful enthusiasm, Rodolfo's intentions towards Catherine are motivated by his love for her. But it is Eddie's reluctance to be displaced in Catherine's affections, as well as his desire for her, which force him to consult Alfieri for advice and which, even after Alfieri has told him to allow events to follow their natural course, force him to betray the brothers to the Immigration Bureau.

This act of betrayal of members of his own extended family brings about the final bloody tragedy which Alfieri foresaw at his first interview with Eddie and which he knew he would be powerless to prevent. For, despite Alfieri's best efforts, Marco is intent upon revenge for his betrayal, while Eddie is determined to maintain his reputation and his honour. They finally come face to face in full view of the neighbourhood and the inevitable tragedy concludes. It is Alfieri, the one character able to reflect objectively on the events of the play, who recognizes that the death of Eddie Carbone should serve as a reminder to those who must carry on, and to the audience, that 'it is better to settle for half, it must be.' Yet, as Alfieri admits, this represents a compromise – of people's hopes, desires and sense of justice – which ultimately he regards with alarm.

Reading the Play

All plays are written to be performed or, at the least, read aloud. This is especially true of *A View from the Bridge* for it is only in reading the dialogue aloud that the nature of the conversational working-class American English can be appreciated. It is not strictly necessary to adopt the same accent, but the rhythms of the dialogue demand an understanding of how the accent dictates some of the sentence structures ('Listen, you been givin' me the willies the way you walk down the street, I mean it'). From this it is possible to develop a sense of how the characters would show their feelings and reactions in other, physical ways. It is only through an effective reading of the play that an understanding of the characters' changes and inter-actions can be reached.

While the play is divided into two acts, various 'scenes' within the acts are easily identifiable and are usually marked by a direct address from Alfieri to the audience. This lends particular sections of the play to detailed study or to reading and rehearsal. A useful approach is to read sections aloud first of all to understand the action and the relationships; then to explore and experiment with the text to discover more depth and understanding of the characters and their developing relationships.

Following the play you will find two series of questions entitled

Keeping Track and *Explorations*. *Keeping Track* is intended to help your understanding of the action and characters as the play develops and can be used when reading the play for the first time. *Explorations* comprises more detailed and demanding questions organized according to character, performance, themes and criticism. The questions in this section may lead to coursework assignments or examination practice. All the questions are designed to stimulate knowledge, understanding and enjoyment of the play

Tim Bezant

List of Characters

A View from the Bridge

A VIEW FROM THE BRIDGE

ACT ONE

The street and house front of a tenement building. The front is skeletal entirely. The main acting area is the living room–dining room of EDDIE'*s apartment. It is a worker's flat, clean, sparse, homely. There is a rocker down front; a round dining table at centre, with chairs; and a portable phonograph.*

At back are a bedroom door and an opening to the kitchen; none of these interiors are seen.

At the right, forestage, a desk. This is MR ALFIERI'*s law office.*

There is also a telephone booth. This is not used until the last scenes, so it may be covered or left in view.

A stairway leads up to the apartment, and then farther up to the next storey which is not seen.

Ramps, representing the street, run upstage and off to right and left.

As the curtain rises, LOUIS *and* MIKE*, longshoremen, are pitching coins against the building at left.*

A distant foghorn blows.

Enter ALFIERI*, a lawyer in his fifties turning gray; he is portly, good-humoured, and thoughtful. The two pitchers nod to him as he passes. He crosses the stage to his desk, removes his hat, runs his fingers through his hair and, grinning, speaks to the audience.*

ALFIERI You wouldn't have known it, but
something amusing has just happened. You see
how uneasily they nod to me? That's because

I am a lawyer. In this neighbourhood to meet a lawyer or a priest on the street is unlucky. We're only thought of in connection with disasters, and they'd rather not get too close.

I often think that behind that suspicious little nod of theirs lie three thousand years of distrust. A lawyer means the law, and in Sicily, from where their fathers came, the law has not been a friendly idea since the Greeks were beaten.

I am inclined to notice the ruins in things, perhaps because I was born in Italy ... I only came here when I was twenty-five. In those days, Al Capone, the greatest Carthaginian of all, was learning his trade on these pavements, and Frankie Yale himself was cut precisely in half by a machine gun on the corner of Union Street, two blocks away. Oh, there were many here who were justly shot by unjust men. Justice is very important here.

But this is Red Hook, not Sicily. This is the slum that faces the bay on the seaward side of Brooklyn Bridge. This is the gullet of New York swallowing the tonnage of the world. And now we are quite civilized, quite American. Now we settle for half, and I like it better. I no longer keep a pistol in my filing cabinet.

And my practice is entirely unromantic.

My wife has warned me, so have my friends; they tell me the people in this neighbourhood lack elegance, glamour. After all, who have I dealt with in my life? Longshoremen and their wives, and fathers and grandfathers, compensation cases, evictions, family squabbles – the petty troubles of the poor – and yet ... every few years there is still a case, and as the parties tell me what the trouble is, the flat air in my office suddenly washes in with the green scent of the sea, the dust in this air is blown away and the thought comes that in some Caesar's year, in Calabria perhaps or on the cliff at Syracuse, another lawyer, quite differently dressed, heard the same complaint and sat there as powerless as I, and watched it run its bloody course.

EDDIE *has appeared and has been pitching coins with the men and is highlighted among them. He is forty – a husky, slightly overweight longshoreman.*

This one's name was Eddie Carbone, a longshoreman working the docks from Brooklyn Bridge to the breakwater where the open sea begins.

ALFIERI *walks into darkness.*

EDDIE   (*moving up steps into doorway*) Well, I'll see ya, fellas.

CATHERINE *enters from kitchen, crosses down to window, looks out.*

LOUIS   You workin' tomorrow?

EDDIE   Yeah, there's another day yet on that ship. See ya, Louis.

EDDIE *goes into the house, as light rises in the apartment.*

CATHERINE *is waving to* LOUIS *from the window and turns to him.*

CATHERINE   Hi, Eddie!

EDDIE *is pleased and therefore shy about it; he hangs up his cap and jacket.*

EDDIE   Where you goin' all dressed up?

CATHERINE   (*running her hands over her skirt*) I just got it. You like it?

EDDIE   Yeah, it's nice. And what happened to your hair?

CATHERINE   You like it? I fixed it different. (*Calling to kitchen*) He's here, B.!

EDDIE   Beautiful. Turn around, lemme see in the back. (*She turns for him.*) Oh, if your mother was alive to see you now! She wouldn't believe it.

CATHERINE   You like it, huh?

EDDIE   You look like one of them girls that went to college. Where you goin'?

CATHERINE   (*taking his arm*) Wait'll B. comes in, I'll tell you something. Here, sit down. (*She is walking him to the armchair. Calling offstage.*) Hurry up, will you, B.?

EDDIE   (*sitting*) What's goin' on?

CATHERINE   I'll get you a beer, all right?

EDDIE   Well, tell me what happened. Come over here, talk to me.

CATHERINE   I want to wait till B. comes in. (*She sits on her heels beside him.*) Guess how much we paid for the skirt.

EDDIE   I think it's too short, ain't it?

CATHERINE   (*standing*) No! not when I stand up.

EDDIE   Yeah, but you gotta sit down sometimes.

CATHERINE   Eddie, it's the style now. (*She walks to show him.*) I mean, if you see me walkin' down the street –

EDDIE	Listen, you been givin' me the willies the way you walk down the street, I mean it.
CATHERINE	Why?
EDDIE	Catherine, I don't want to be a pest, but I'm tellin' you you're walkin' wavy.
CATHERINE	I'm walkin' wavy?
EDDIE	Now don't aggravate me, Katie, you are walkin' wavy! I don't like the looks they're givin' you in the candy store. And with them new high heels on the sidewalk – clack, clack, clack. The heads are turnin' like windmills.
CATHERINE	But those guys look at all the girls, you know that.
EDDIE	You ain't 'all the girls'.
CATHERINE	(*almost in tears because he disapproves*) What do you want me to do? You want me to –
EDDIE	Now don't get mad, kid.
CATHERINE	Well, I don't know what you want from me.
EDDIE	Katie, I promised your mother on her deathbed. I'm responsible for you. You're a baby, you don't understand these things. I mean like when you stand here by the window, wavin' outside.
CATHERINE	I was wavin' to Louis!
EDDIE	Listen, I could tell you things about Louis which you wouldn't wave to him no more.
CATHERINE	(*trying to joke him out of his warning*) Eddie, I wish there was one guy you couldn't tell me things about!
EDDIE	Catherine, do me a favour, will you? You're gettin' to be a big girl now, you gotta keep yourself more, you can't be so friendly, kid. (*Calls*) Hey, B., what're you doin' in there? (*To* CATHERINE) Get her in here, will you! I got news for her.
CATHERINE	(*starting out*) What?
EDDIE	Her cousins landed.
CATHERINE	(*clapping her hands together*) No! (*She turns instantly and starts for the kitchen.*) B.! Your cousins!
	BEATRICE *enters, wiping her hands with a towel.*
BEATRICE	(*in the face of* CATHERINE *'s shout*) What?
CATHERINE	Your cousins got in!
BEATRICE	(*astounded, turns to* EDDIE) What are you talkin' about? Where?

EDDIE	I was just knockin' off work before and Tony Bereli come over to me; he says the ship is in the North River.
BEATRICE	(*her hands are clasped at her breast; she seems half in fear, half in unutterable joy*) They're all right?
EDDIE	He didn't see them yet, they're still on board. But as soon as they get off he'll meet them. He figures about ten o'clock they'll be here.
BEATRICE	(*sits, almost weak from tension*) And they'll let them off the ship all right? That's fixed, heh?
EDDIE	Sure, they give them regular seamen papers and they walk off with the crew. Don't worry about it, B., there's nothin' to it. Couple of hours they'll be here.
BEATRICE	What happened? They wasn't supposed to be till next Thursday.
EDDIE	I don't know; they put them on any ship they can get them out on. Maybe the other ship they was supposed to take there was some danger – What you cryin' about?
BEATRICE	(*astounded and afraid*) I'm – I just – I can't believe it! I didn't even buy a new tablecloth; I was gonna wash the walls –
EDDIE	Listen, they'll think it's a millionaire's house compared to the way they live. Don't worry about the walls. They'll be thankful. (*To* CATHERINE) Whyn't you run down buy a table-cloth. Go ahead, here. (*He is reaching into his pocket.*)
CATHERINE	There's no stores open now.
EDDIE	(*To* BEATRICE) You was gonna put a new cover on the chair.
BEATRICE	I know – well, I thought it was gonna be next week! I was gonna clean the walls, I was gonna wax the floors. (*She stands disturbed.*)
CATHERINE	(*pointing upward*) Maybe Mrs Dondero upstairs –
BEATRICE	(*of the tablecloth*) No, hers is worse than this one. (*Suddenly*) My God, I don't even have nothin' to eat for them! (*She starts for the kitchen.*)
EDDIE	(*reaching out and grabbing her arm*) Hey, hey! Take it easy.
BEATRICE	No, I'm just nervous, that's all. (*To* CATHERINE) I'll make the fish.
EDDIE	You're savin' their lives, what're you worryin' about the table cloth? They probably didn't see a table-cloth in their whole life where they come from.

BEATRICE   (*looking into his eyes*) I'm just worried about you, that's all
         I'm worried.

EDDIE   Listen, as long as they know where they're gonna sleep.

BEATRICE   I told them in the letters. They're sleepin' on the floor.

EDDIE   Beatrice, all I'm worried about is you got such a heart that
         I'll end up on the floor with you, and they'll be in our bed.

BEATRICE   All right, stop it.

EDDIE   Because as soon as you see a tired relative, I end up on the
         floor.

BEATRICE   When did you end up on the floor?

EDDIE   When your father's house burned down I didn't end up on
         the floor.

BEATRICE   Well, their house burned down!

EDDIE   Yeah, but it didn't keep burnin' for two weeks!

BEATRICE   All right, look, I'll tell them to go someplace else. (*She starts
         into the kitchen.*)

EDDIE   Now wait a minute. Beatrice! (*She halts. He goes to her.*) I
         just don't want you bein' pushed around, that's all. You got
         too big a heart. (*He touches her hand.*) What're you so
         touchy?

BEATRICE   I'm just afraid if it don't turn out good you'll be mad at me.

EDDIE   Listen, if everybody keeps his mouth shut, nothin' can
         happen. They'll pay for their board.

BEATRICE   Oh, I told them.

EDDIE   Then what the hell. (*Pause. He moves.*) It's an honour, B., I
         mean it. I was just thinkin' before, comin' home, suppose
         my father didn't come to this country, and I was starvin' like
         them over there ... and I had people in America could keep
         me a couple of months? The man would be honoured to
         lend me a place to sleep.

BEATRICE   (*there are tears in her eyes; she turns to* CATHERINE) You see
         what he is? (*She turns and grabs* EDDIE*'s face in her hands.*)
         Mmm! You're an angel! God'll bless you. (*He is gratefully
         smiling.*) You'll see, you'll get a blessing for this!

EDDIE   (*laughing*) I'll settle for my own bed.

BEATRICE   Go, Baby, set the table.

CATHERINE   We didn't tell him about me yet.

BEATRICE   Let him eat first, then we'll tell him. Bring everything in.
         (*She hurries* CATHERINE *out.*)

EDDIE	(*sitting at the table*) What's all that about? Where's she goin'?
BEATRICE	Noplace. It's very good news, Eddie. I want you to be happy.
EDDIE	What's goin' on?
	CATHERINE *enters with plates, forks.*
BEATRICE	She's got a job.
	Pause. EDDIE *looks at* CATHERINE, *then back to* BEATRICE.
EDDIE	What job? She's gonna finish school.
CATHERINE	Eddie, you won't believe it –
EDDIE	No – no, you gonna finish school. What kinda job, what do you mean? All of a sudden you –
CATHERINE	Listen a minute, it's wonderful.
EDDIE	It's not wonderful. You'll never get nowheres unless you finish school. You can't take no job. Why didn't you ask me before you take a job?
BEATRICE	She's askin' you now, she didn't take nothin' yet.
CATHERINE	Listen a minute! I came to school this morning and the principal called me out of the class, see? To go to his office.
EDDIE	Yeah?
CATHERINE	So I went in and he says to me he's got my records, y'know? And there's a company wants a girl right away. It ain't exactly a secretary, it's a stenographer first, but pretty soon you get to be secretary. And he says to me that I'm the best student in the whole class –
BEATRICE	You hear that?
EDDIE	Well why not? Sure she's the best.
CATHERINE	I'm the best student, he says, and if I want, I should take the job and the end of the year he'll let me take the examination and he'll give me the certificate. So I'll save practically a year!
EDDIE	(*strangely nervous*) Where's the job? What company?
CATHERINE	It's a big plumbing company over Nostrand Avenue.
EDDIE	Nostrand Avenue and where?
CATHERINE	It's someplace by the Navy Yard.
BEATRICE	Fifty dollars a week, Eddie.
EDDIE	(*to* CATHERINE, *surprised*) Fifty?
CATHERINE	I swear.
	Pause.

EDDIE	What about all the stuff you wouldn't learn this year, though?
CATHERINE	There's nothin' more to learn, Eddie, I just gotta practise from now on. I know all the symbols and I know the keyboard. I'll just get faster, that's all. And when I'm workin' I'll keep gettin' better and better, you see?
BEATRICE	Work is the best practice anyway.
EDDIE	That ain't what I wanted, though.
CATHERINE	Why! It's a great big company –
EDDIE	I don't like the neighbourhood over there.
CATHERINE	It's a block and a half from the subway, he says.
EDDIE	Near the Navy Yard plenty can happen in a block and a half. And a plumbin' company! That's one step over the water front. They're practically longshoremen.
BEATRICE	Yeah, but she'll be in the office, Eddie.
EDDIE	I know she'll be in the office, but that ain't what I had in mind.
BEATRICE	Listen, she's gotta go to work sometime.
EDDIE	Listen, B., she'll be with a lotta plumbers? And sailors up and down the street? So what did she go to school for?
CATHERINE	But it's fifty a week, Eddie.
EDDIE	Look, did I ask you for money? I supported you this long I support you a little more. Please, do me a favour, will ya? I want you to be with different kind of people. I want you to be in a nice office. Maybe a lawyer's office someplace in New York in one of them nice buildings. I mean if you're gonna get outa here then get out; don't go practically in the same kind of neighbourhood.
	Pause. CATHERINE *lowers her eyes.*
BEATRICE	Go, Baby, bring in the supper. (CATHERINE *goes out.*) Think about it a little bit, Eddie. Please. She's crazy to start work. It's not a little shop, it's a big company. Some day she could be a secretary. They picked her out of the whole class. (*He is silent, staring down at the tablecloth, fingering the pattern.*) What are you worried about? She could take care of herself. She'll get out of the subway and be in the office in two minutes.
EDDIE	(*somehow sickened*) I know that neighbourhood, B., I don't like it.

BEATRICE   Listen, if nothin' happened to her in this neighbourhood it ain't gonna happen noplace else. (*She turns his face to her.*) Look, you gotta get used to it, she's no baby no more. Tell her to take it. (*He turns his head away.*) You hear me? (*She is angering.*) I don't understand you; she's seventeen years old, you gonna keep her in the house all her life?

EDDIE   (*insulted*) What kinda remark is that?

BEATRICE   (*with sympathy but insistent force*) Well, I don't understand when it ends. First it was gonna be when she graduated high school, so she graduated high school. Then it was gonna be when she learned stenographer, so she learned stenographer. So what're we gonna wait for now? I mean it, Eddie, sometimes I don't understand you; they picked her out of the whole class, it's an honour for her.

CATHERINE *enters with food, which she silently sets on the table. After a moment of watching her face,* EDDIE *breaks into a smile, but it almost seems that tears will form in his eyes.*

EDDIE   With your hair that way you look like a madonna, you know that? You're the madonna type. (*She doesn't look at him, but continues ladling out food onto the plates.*) You wanna go to work, heh, Madonna?

CATHERINE   (*softly*) Yeah.

EDDIE   (*with a sense of her childhood, her babyhood, and the years*) All right, go to work. (*She looks at him, then rushes and hugs him.*) Hey, hey! Take it easy! (*He holds her face away from him to look at her.*) What're you cryin' about? (*He is affected by her, but smiles his emotion away.*)

CATHERINE   (*sitting at her place*) I just – (*Bursting out*) I'm gonna buy all new dishes with my first pay! (*They laugh warmly.*) I mean it. I'll fix up the whole house! I'll buy a rug!

EDDIE   And then you'll move away.

CATHERINE   No, Eddie!

EDDIE   (*grinning*) Why not? That's life. And you'll come visit on Sundays, then once a month, then Christmas and New Year's, finally.

CATHERINE   (*grasping his arm to reassure him and to erase the accusation*) No, please!

EDDIE   (*smiling but hurt*) I only ask you one thing – don't trust nobody. You got a good aunt but she's got too big a heart, you learned bad from her. Believe me.

BEATRICE Be the way you are, Katie, don't listen to him.

EDDIE (*to* BEATRICE – *strangely and quickly resentful*) You lived in a house all your life, what do you know about it? You never worked in your life.

BEATRICE She likes people. What's wrong with that?

EDDIE Because most people ain't people. She's goin' to work; plumbers; they'll chew her to pieces if she don't watch out. (*To* CATHERINE) Believe me, Katie, the less you trust, the less you be sorry.

EDDIE *crosses himself and the women do the same, and they eat.*

CATHERINE First thing I'll buy is a rug, heh, B.?

BEATRICE I don't mind. (*To* EDDIE) I smelled coffee all day today. You unloadin' coffee today?

EDDIE Yeah, a Brazil ship.

CATHERINE I smelled it too. It smelled all over the neighbourhood.

EDDIE That's one time, boy, to be a longshoreman is a pleasure. I could work coffee ships twenty hours a day. You go down in the hold, y'know? It's like flowers, that smell. We'll bust a bag tomorrow, I'll bring you some.

BEATRICE Just be sure there's no spiders in it, will ya? I mean it. (*She directs this to* CATHERINE, *rolling her eyes upward.*) I still remember that spider coming out of that bag he brung home. I nearly died.

EDDIE You call that a spider? You oughta see what comes outa the bananas sometimes.

BEATRICE Don't talk about it!

EDDIE I seen spiders could stop a Buick.

BEATRICE (*clapping her hands over her ears*) All right, shut up!

EDDIE (*laughing and taking a watch out of his pocket*) Well, who started with spiders?

BEATRICE All right, I'm sorry. I didn't mean it. Just don't bring none home again. What time is it?

EDDIE Quarter nine. (*Puts watch back in his pocket.*)

They continue eating in silence.

CATHERINE He's bringin' them ten o'clock, Tony?

EDDIE   Around, yeah. (*He eats.*)

CATHERINE   Eddie, suppose somebody asks if they're livin' here. (*He looks at her as though already she had divulged something publicly. Defensively*) I mean if they ask.

EDDIE   Now look, Baby, I can see we're gettin' mixed up again here.

CATHERINE   No, I just mean ... people'll see them goin' in and out.

EDDIE   I don't care who sees them goin' in and out as long as you don't see them goin' in and out. And this goes for you too, B. You don't see nothin' and you don't know nothin'.

BEATRICE   What do you mean? I understand.

EDDIE   You don't understand; you still think you can talk about this to somebody just a little bit. Now lemme say it once and for all, because you're makin' me nervous again, both of you. I don't care if somebody comes in the house and sees them sleepin' on the floor, it never comes out of your mouth who they are or what they're doin' here.

BEATRICE   Yeah, but my mother'll know –

EDDIE   Sure she'll know, but just don't be the one who told her, that's all. This is the United States government you're playin' with now, this is the Immigration Bureau. If you said it you knew it, if you didn't say it you didn't know it.

CATHERINE   Yeah, but Eddie, suppose somebody –

EDDIE   I don't care what question it is. You – don't – know – nothin'. They got stool pigeons all over this neighbourhood they're payin' them every week for information, and you don't know who they are. It could be your best friend. You hear? (*To* BEATRICE) Like Vinny Bolzano, remember Vinny?

BEATRICE   Oh, yeah. God forbid.

EDDIE   Tell her about Vinny. (*To* CATHERINE) You think I'm blowin' steam here? (*To* BEATRICE) Go ahead, tell her. (*To* CATHERINE) You was a baby then. There was a family lived next door to her mother, he was about sixteen –

BEATRICE   No, he was no more than fourteen, cause I was to his confirmation in Saint Agnes. But the family had an uncle that they were hidin' in the house, and he snitched to the Immigration.

CATHERINE   The kid snitched?

EDDIE	On his own uncle!
CATHERINE	What, was he crazy?
EDDIE	He was crazy after, I tell you that, boy.
BEATRICE	Oh, it was terrible. He had five brothers and the old father. And they grabbed him in the kitchen and pulled him down the stairs – three flights his head was bouncin' like a coconut. And they spit on him in the street, his own father and his brothers. The whole neighbourhood was cryin'.
CATHERINE	Ts! So what happened to him?
BEATRICE	I think he went away. (*To* EDDIE) I never seen him again, did you?
EDDIE	(*rises during this, taking out his watch*) Him? You'll never see him no more, a guy do a thing like that? How's he gonna show his face? (*To* CATHERINE, *as he gets up uneasily*) Just remember, kid, you can quicker get back a million dollars that was stole than a word that you gave away. (*He is standing now, stretching his back.*)
CATHERINE	Okay, I won't say a word to nobody, I swear.
EDDIE	Gonna rain tomorrow. We'll be slidin' all over the decks. Maybe you oughta put something on for them, they be here soon.
BEATRICE	I only got fish, I hate to spoil it if they ate already. I'll wait, it only takes a few minutes; I could broil it.
CATHERINE	What happens, Eddie, when that ship pulls out and they ain't on it, though? Don't the captain say nothin'?
EDDIE	(*slicing an apple with his pocket knife*) Captain's pieced off, what do you mean?
CATHERINE	Even the captain?
EDDIE	What's the matter, the captain don't have to live? Captain gets a piece, maybe one of the mates, piece for the guy in Italy who fixed the papers for them, Tony here'll get a little bite. ...
BEATRICE	I just hope they get work here, that's all I hope.
EDDIE	Oh, the syndicate'll fix jobs for them; till they pay 'em off they'll get them work every day. It's after the pay-off, then they'll have to scramble like the rest of us.
BEATRICE	Well, it be better than they got there.
EDDIE	Oh sure, well, listen. So you gonna start Monday, heh, Madonna?
CATHERINE	(*embarrassed*) I'm supposed to, yeah.

EDDIE *is standing facing the two seated women. First* BEATRICE *smiles, then* CATHERINE, *for a powerful emotion is on him, a childish one and a knowing fear, and the tears show in his eyes – and they are shy before the avowal.*

EDDIE   (*sadly smiling, yet somehow proud of her*) Well … I hope you have good luck. I wish you the best. You know that, kid.

CATHERINE   (*rising, trying to laugh*) You sound like I'm goin' a million miles!

EDDIE   I know. I guess I just never figured on one thing.

CATHERINE   (*smiling*) What?

EDDIE   That you would ever grow up. (*He utters a soundless laugh at himself, feeling his breast pocket of his shirt.*) I left a cigar in my other coat, I think. (*He starts for the bedroom.*)

CATHERINE   Stay there! I'll get it for you.

She hurries out. There is a slight pause, and EDDIE *turns to* BEATRICE, *who has been avoiding his gaze.*

EDDIE   What are you mad at me lately?

BEATRICE   Who's mad? (*She gets up, clearing the dishes.*) I'm not mad. (*She picks up the dishes and turns to him.*) You're the one is mad. (*She turns and goes into the kitchen as* CATHERINE *enters from the bedroom with a cigar and a pack of matches.*)

CATHERINE   Here! I'll light it for you! (*She strikes a match and holds it to his cigar. He puffs. Quietly*) Don't worry about me, Eddie, heh?

EDDIE   Don't burn yourself. (*Just in time she blows out the match.*) You better go in help her with the dishes.

CATHERINE   (*turns quickly to the table, and, seeing the table cleared, she says, almost guiltily*) Oh! (*She hurries into the kitchen, and as she exits there*) I'll do the dishes, B.!

Alone, EDDIE *stands looking toward the kitchen for a moment. Then he takes out his watch, glances at it, replaces it in his pocket, sits in the armchair, and stares at the smoke flowing out of his mouth.*

The lights go down, then come up on ALFIERI, *who has moved onto the forestage.*

ALFIERI   He was as good a man as he had to be in a life that was hard and even. He worked on the piers when there was work, he brought home his pay, and he lived. And toward ten o'clock of that night, after they had eaten, the cousins came.

The lights fade on ALFIERI *and rise on the street.*

Enter TONY, *escorting* MARCO *and* RODOLFO, *each with a valise.*
TONY *halts, indicates the house. They stand for a moment
looking at it.*

MARCO (*he is a square-built peasant of thirty-two, suspicious, tender,
and quiet-voiced*) Thank you.

TONY You're on your own now. Just be careful, that's all. Ground
floor.

MARCO Thank you.

TONY (*indicating the house*) I'll see you on the pier tomorrow.
You'll go to work.

MARCO *nods.* TONY *continues on walking down the street.*

RODOLFO This will be the first house I ever walked into in America!
Imagine! She said they were poor!

MARCO Ssh! Come. (*They go to door.*)

MARCO *knocks. The lights rise in the room.* EDDIE *goes and
opens the door. Enter* MARCO *and* RODOLFO, *removing their
caps.* BEATRICE *and* CATHERINE *enter from the kitchen. The
lights fade in the street.*

EDDIE You Marco?

MARCO Marco.

EDDIE Come on in! (*He shakes* MARCO'*s hand.*)

BEATRICE Here, take the bags!

MARCO (*nods, looks to the women and fixes on* BEATRICE. *Crosses to*
BEATRICE) Are you my cousin?

She nods. He kisses her hand.

BEATRICE (*above the table, touching her chest with her hand*) Beatrice.
This is my husband Eddie. (*All nod.*) Catherine, my sister
Nancy's daughter. (*The brothers nod.*)

MARCO (*indicating* RODOLFO) My brother. Rodolfo. (RODOLFO *nods.*
MARCO *comes with a certain formal stiffness to* EDDIE). I want
to tell you now Eddie – when you say go, we will go.

EDDIE Oh, no … (*Takes* MARCO'*s bag.*)

MARCO I see it's a small house, but soon, maybe, we can have our
own house.

EDDIE You're welcome, Marco, we got plenty of room here. Katie,
give them supper, heh? (*Exits into bedroom with their bags.*)

MARCO (*as they go to the table*) We ate on the ship. Thank you. (*To*
EDDIE, *calling off to bedroom*) Thank you.

BEATRICE	Get some coffee. We'll all have coffee. Come sit down.
	RODOLFO *and* MARCO *sit, at the table.*
CATHERINE	(*wondrously*) How come he's so dark and you're so light, Rodolfo?
RODOLFO	(*ready to laugh*) I don't know. A thousand years ago, they say, the Danes invaded Sicily.
	BEATRICE *kisses* RODOLFO. *They laugh as* EDDIE *enters.*
CATHERINE	(*to* BEATRICE) He's practically blond!
EDDIE	How's the coffee doin'?
CATHERINE	(*brought up*) I'm gettin' it. (*She hurries out to kitchen.*)
EDDIE	(*sits on his rocker*) Yiz have a nice trip?
MARCO	The ocean is always rough. But we are good sailors.
EDDIE	No trouble gettin' here?
MARCO	No. The man brought us. Very nice man.
RODOLFO	(*to* EDDIE) He says we start to work tomorrow. Is he honest?
EDDIE	(*laughing*) No. But as long as you owe them money, they'll get you plenty of work. (*To* MARCO) Yiz ever work on the piers in Italy?
MARCO	Piers? Ts! – no.
RODOLFO	(*smiling at the smallness of his town*) In our town there are no piers, only the beach, and little fishing boats.
BEATRICE	So what kinda work did yiz do?
MARCO	(*shrugging shyly, even embarrassed*) Whatever there is, anything.
RODOLFO	Sometimes they build a house, or if they fix the bridge – Marco is a mason and I bring him the cement. (*He laughs.*) In harvest time we work in the fields ... if there is work. Anything.
EDDIE	Still bad there, heh?
MARCO	Bad, yes.
RODOLFO	(*laughing*) It's terrible! We stand around all day in the piazza listening to the fountain like birds. Everybody waits only for the train.
BEATRICE	What's on the train?
RODOLFO	Nothing. But if there are many passengers and you're lucky you make a few lire to push the taxi up the hill.
	Enter CATHERINE; *she listens.*
BEATRICE	You gotta push a taxi?

RODOLFO	(*laughing*) Oh, sure! It's a feature in our town. The horses in our town are skinnier than goats. So if there are too many passengers we help to push the carriages up to the hotel. (*He laughs.*) In our town the horses are only for show.
CATHERINE	Why don't they have automobile taxis?
RODOLFO	There is one. We push that too. (*They laugh.*) Everything in our town, you gotta push!
BEATRICE	(*to* EDDIE) How do you like that?
EDDIE	(*to* MARCO) So what're you wanna do, you gonna stay here in this country or you wanna go back?
MARCO	(*surprised*) Go back?
EDDIE	Well, you're married, ain't you?
MARCO	Yes. I have three children.
BEATRICE	Three! I thought only one.
MARCO	Oh, no. I have three now. Four years, five years, six years.
BEATRICE	Ah … I bet they're cryin' for you already, heh?
MARCO	What can I do? The older one is sick in his chest. My wife – she feeds them from her own mouth. I tell you the truth, if I stay there they will never grow up. They eat the sunshine.
BEATRICE	My God. So how long you want to stay?
MARCO	With your permission, we will stay maybe a –
EDDIE	She don't mean in this house, she means in the country.
MARCO	Oh. Maybe four, five, six years, I think.
RODOLFO	(*smiling*) He trusts his wife.
BEATRICE	Yeah, but maybe you'll get enough, you'll be able to go back quicker.
MARCO	I hope. I don't know. (*To* EDDIE) I understand it's not so good here either.
EDDIE	Oh, you guys'll be all right – till you pay them off, anyway. After that, you'll have to scramble, that's all. But you'll make better here than you could there.
RODOLFO	How much? We hear all kinds of figures. How much can a man make? We work hard, we'll work all day, all night –
	MARCO *raises a hand to hush him.*
EDDIE	(*he is coming more and more to address* MARCO *only*) On the average a whole year? Maybe – well, it's hard to say, see. Sometimes we lay off, there's no ships three four weeks.

MARCO	Three, four weeks! – Ts!
EDDIE	But I think you could probably – thirty, forty a week, over the whole twelve months of the year.
MARCO	(*rises, crosses to* EDDIE) Dollars.
EDDIE	Sure dollars.

MARCO *puts an arm round* RODOLFO *and they laugh.*

MARCO	If we can stay here a few months, Beatrice –
BEATRICE	Listen, you're welcome, Marco –
MARCO	Because I could send them a little more if I stay here.
BEATRICE	As long as you want, we got plenty a room.
MARCO	(*his eyes are showing tears*) My wife – (*To* EDDIE) My wife – I want to send right away maybe twenty dollars –
EDDIE	You could send them something next week already.
MARCO	(*he is near tears*) Eduardo … (*He goes to* EDDIE, *offering his hand.*)
EDDIE	Don't thank me. Listen, what the hell, it's no skin off me. (*To* CATHERINE) What happened to the coffee?
CATHERINE	I got it on. (*To* RODOLFO) You married too? No.
RODOLFO	(*rises*) Oh, no …
BEATRICE	(*to* CATHERINE) I told you he –
CATHERINE	I know, I just thought maybe he got married recently.
RODOLFO	I have no money to get married. I have a nice face, but no money. (*He laughs.*)
CATHERINE	(*to* BEATRICE) He's a real blond!
BEATRICE	(*to* RODOLFO) You want to stay here too, heh? For good?
RODOLFO	Me? Yes, forever! Me, I want to be an American. And then I want to go back to Italy when I am rich, and I will buy a motorcycle. (*He smiles.* MARCO *shakes him affectionately.*)
CATHERINE	A motorcycle!
RODOLFO	With a motorcycle in Italy you will never starve any more.
BEATRICE	I'll get you coffee. (*She exits to the kitchen.*)
EDDIE	What you do with a motorcycle?
MARCO	He dreams, he dreams.
RODOLFO	(*to* MARCO) Why? (*To* EDDIE) Messages! The rich people in the hotel always need someone who will carry a message. But quickly, and with a great noise. With a blue motorcycle I would

station myself in the courtyard of the hotel, and in a little
while I would have messages.

MARCO When you have no wife you have dreams.

EDDIE Why can't you just walk, or take a trolley or sump'm?

Enter BEATRICE *with coffee.*

RODOLFO Oh, no, the machine, the machine is necessary. A man comes
into a great hotel and says, I am a messenger. Who is this
man? He disappears walking, there is no noise, nothing.
Maybe he will never come back, maybe he will never deliver
the message. But a man who rides up on a great machine,
this man is responsible, this man exists. He will be given
messages. (*He helps* BEATRICE *set out the coffee things.*) I am
also a singer, though.

EDDIE You mean a regular – ?

RODOLFO Oh, yes. One night last year Andreola got sick. Baritone. And
I took his place in the garden of the hotel. Three arias I sang
without a mistake! Thousand-lire notes they threw from the
tables, money was falling like a storm in the treasury. It was
magnificent. We lived six months on that night, eh, Marco?

MARCO *nods doubtfully.*

MARCO Two months.

EDDIE *laughs.*

BEATRICE Can't you get a job in that place?

RODOLFO Andreola got better. He's a baritone, very strong.

BEATRICE *laughs.*

MARCO (*regretfully, to* BEATRICE) He sang too loud.

RODOLFO Why too loud?

MARCO Too loud. The guests in that hotel are all Englishmen. They
don't like too loud.

RODOLFO (*to* CATHERINE) Nobody ever said it was too loud!

MARCO I say. It was too loud. (*To* BEATRICE) I knew it as soon as he
started to sing. Too loud.

RODOLFO Then why did they throw so much money?

MARCO They paid for your courage. The English like courage. But
once is enough.

RODOLFO (*to all but* MARCO) I never heard anybody say it was too loud.

CATHERINE Did you ever hear of jazz?

RODOLFO Oh, sure! I *sing* jazz.

CATHERINE	(*rises*) You could sing jazz?
RODOLFO	Oh, I sing Napolidan, jazz, bel canto – I sing 'Paper Doll', you like 'Paper Doll'?
CATHERINE	Oh, sure, I'm crazy for 'Paper Doll'. Go ahead, sing it.
RODOLFO	(*takes his stance after getting a nod of permission from* MARCO, *and with a high tenor voice begins singing:*

'I'll tell you boys it's tough to be alone,
And it's tough to love a doll that's not your own.
I'm through with all of them,
I'll never fall again,
Hey, boy, what you gonna do?
I'm gonna buy a paper doll that I can call my own,
A doll that other fellows cannot steal.

EDDIE *rises and moves upstage.*

And then those flirty, flirty guys
With their flirty, flirty eyes
Will have to flirt with dollies that are real –

EDDIE	Hey, kid – hey, wait a minute –
CATHERINE	(*enthralled*) Leave him finish, it's beautiful! (*To* BEATRICE) He's terrific! It's terrific, Rodolfo.
EDDIE	Look, kid; you don't want to be picked up, do ya?
MARCO	No – no! (*He rises.*)
EDDIE	(*indicating the rest of the building*) Because we never had no singers here ... and all of a sudden there's a singer in the house, y'know what I mean?
MARCO	Yes, yes. You'll be quiet, Rodolfo.
EDDIE	(*he is flushed*) They got guys all over the place, Marco. I mean.
MARCO	Yes. He'll be quiet. (*To* RODOLFO) You'll be quiet.

RODOLFO *nods.*

EDDIE *has risen, with iron control, even a smile. He moves to* CATHERINE.

EDDIE	What's the high heels for, Garbo?
CATHERINE	I figured for tonight –
EDDIE	Do me a favour, will you? Go ahead.

Embarrassed now, angered, CATHERINE *goes out into the bedroom.* BEATRICE *watches her go and gets up; in passing, she gives* EDDIE *a cold look, restrained only by the strangers, and goes to the table to pour coffee.*

EDDIE (*striving to laugh, and to* MARCO, *but directed as much to* BEATRICE) All actresses they want to be around here.

RODOLFO (*happy about it*) In Italy too! All the girls.

CATHERINE emerges from the bedroom in low-heel shoes, comes to the table. RODOLFO *is lifting a cup.*

EDDIE (*he is sizing up* RODOLFO, *and there is a concealed suspicion*) Yeah, heh?

RODOLFO Yes! (*Laughs, indicating* CATHERINE) Especially when they are so beautiful!

CATHERINE You like sugar?

RODOLFO Sugar? Yes! I like sugar very much!

EDDIE is downstage, watching as she pours a spoonful of sugar into his cup, his face puffed with trouble, and the room dies.

Lights rise on ALFIERI.

ALFIERI Who can ever know what will be discovered? Eddie Carbone had never expected to have a destiny. A man works, raises his family, goes bowling, eats, gets old, and then he dies. Now, as the weeks passed, there was a future, there was a trouble that would not go away.

The lights fade on ALFIERI, *then rise on* EDDIE *standing at the doorway of the house.* BEATRICE *enters on the street. She sees* EDDIE, *smiles at him. He looks away.*

She starts to enter the house when EDDIE *speaks.*

EDDIE It's after eight.

BEATRICE Well, it's a long show at the Paramount.

EDDIE They must've seen every picture in Brooklyn by now. He's supposed to stay in the house when he ain't working. He ain't supposed to go advertising himself.

BEATRICE Well that's his trouble, what do you care? If they pick him up they pick him up, that's all. Come in the house.

EDDIE What happened to the stenography? I don't see her practise no more.

BEATRICE She'll get back to it. She's excited, Eddie.

EDDIE She tell you anything?

BEATRICE (*comes to him, now the subject is opened*) What's the matter with you? He's a nice kid, what do you want from him?

EDDIE	That's a nice kid? He gives me the heeby-jeebies.
BEATRICE	(*smiling*) Ah, go on, you're just jealous.
EDDIE	Of *him*? Boy, you don't think much of me.
BEATRICE	I don't understand you. What's so terrible about him?
EDDIE	You mean it's all right with you? That's gonna be her husband?
BEATRICE	Why? He's a nice fella, hard workin', he's a good-lookin' fella.
EDDIE	He sings on the ships, didja know that?
BEATRICE	What do you mean, he sings?
EDDIE	Just what I said, he sings. Right on the deck, all of a sudden, a whole song comes out of his mouth – with motions. You know what they're callin' him now? Paper Doll they're callin' him, Canary. He's like a weird. He comes out on the pier, one-two-three, it's a regular free show.
BEATRICE	Well, he's a kid; he don't know how to behave himself yet.
EDDIE	And with that wacky hair; he's like a chorus girl or sump'm.
BEATRICE	So he's blond, so –
EDDIE	I just hope that's his regular hair, that's all I hope.
BEATRICE	You crazy or sump'm? (*She tries to turn him to her.*)
EDDIE	(*he keeps his head turned away*) What's so crazy? I don't like his whole way.
BEATRICE	Listen, you never seen a blond guy in your life? What about Whitey Balso?
EDDIE	(*turning to her victoriously*) Sure, but Whitey don't sing; he don't do that on the ships.
BEATRICE	Well, maybe that's the way they do in Italy.
EDDIE	Then why don't his brother sing? Marco goes around like a man; nobody kids Marco. (*He moves from her, halts. She realizes there is a campaign solidified in him.*) I tell you the truth I'm surprised I have to tell you all this. I mean I'm surprised, B.
BEATRICE	(*she goes to him with purpose now*) Listen, you ain't gonna start nothin' here.
EDDIE	I ain't startin' nothin', but I ain't gonna stand around lookin' at that. For that character I didn't bring her up. I swear, B., I'm surprised at you; I sit there waitin' for you to wake up but everything is great with you.

BEATRICE No, everything ain't great with me.

EDDIE No?

BEATRICE No. But I got other worries.

EDDIE Yeah. (*He is already weakening.*)

BEATRICE Yeah, you want me to tell you?

EDDIE (*in retreat*) Why? What worries you got?

BEATRICE When am I gonna be a wife again, Eddie?

EDDIE I ain't been feelin' good. They bother me since they came.

BEATRICE It's almost three months you don't feel good; they're only here a couple of weeks. It's three months, Eddie.

EDDIE I don't know, B. I don't want to talk about it.

BEATRICE What's the matter, Eddie, you don't like me, heh?

EDDIE What do you mean, I don't like you? I said I don't feel good, that's all.

BEATRICE Well, tell me, am I doing something wrong? Talk to me.

EDDIE (*Pause. He can't speak, then*) I can't. I can't talk about it.

BEATRICE Well tell me what –

EDDIE I got nothin' to say about it!

She stands for a moment; he is looking off; she turns to go into the house.

EDDIE I'll be all right, B.; just lay off me, will ya? I'm worried about her.

BEATRICE The girl is gonna be eighteen years old, it's time already.

EDDIE B., he's taking her for a ride!

BEATRICE All right, that's her ride. What're you gonna stand over her till she's forty? Eddie, I want you to cut it out now, you hear me? I don't like it! Now come in the house.

EDDIE I want to take a walk, I'll be in right away.

BEATRICE They ain't goin' to come any quicker if you stand in the street. It ain't nice, Eddie.

EDDIE I'll be in right away. Go ahead. (*He walks off.*)

She goes into the house. EDDIE *glances up the street, sees* LOUIS *and* MIKE *coming, and sits on an iron railing.* LOUIS *and* MIKE *enter.*

LOUIS Wanna go bowlin' tonight?

EDDIE I'm too tired. Goin' to sleep.

LOUIS How's your two submarines?

EDDIE	They're okay.
LOUIS	I see they're gettin' work allatime.
EDDIE	Oh yeah, they're doin' all right.
MIKE	That's what we oughta do. We oughta leave the country and come in under the water. Then we get work.
EDDIE	You ain't kiddin'.
LOUIS	Well, what the hell. Y'know?
EDDIE	Sure.
LOUIS	(*sits on railing beside* EDDIE) Believe me, Eddie, you got a lotta credit comin' to you.
EDDIE	Aah, they don't bother me, don't cost me nutt'n.
MIKE	That older one, boy, he's a regular bull. I seen him the other day liftin' coffee bags over the Matson Line. They leave him alone he woulda load the whole ship by himself.
EDDIE	Yeah, he's a strong guy, that guy. Their father was a regular giant, supposed to be.
LOUIS	Yeah, you could see. He's a regular slave.
MIKE	(*grinning*) That blond one, though – (EDDIE *looks at him*.) He's got a sense of humour. (LOUIS *snickers*.)
EDDIE	(*searchingly*) Yeah. He's funny –
MIKE	(*starting to laugh*) Well he ain't exackly funny, but he's always like makin' remarks like, y'know? He comes around, everybody's laughin', (LOUIS *laughs*.)
EDDIE	(*uncomfortably, grinning*) Yeah, well … he's got a sense of humour.
MIKE	(*laughing*) Yeah, I mean, he's always makin' like remarks, like, y'know?
EDDIE	Yeah, I know. But he's a kid yet, y'know? He – he's just a kid, that's all.
MIKE	(*getting hysterical with* LOUIS) I know. You take one look at him – everybody's happy. (LOUIS *laughs*.) I worked one day with him last week over the Moore–MacCormack Line, I'm tellin' you they was all hysterical. (LOUIS *and he explode in laughter*.)
EDDIE	Why? What'd he do?
MIKE	I don't know … he was just humorous. You never can remember what he says, y'know? But it's the way he says it. I mean he gives you a look sometimes and you start laughin'!
EDDIE	Yeah. (*Troubled*) He's got a sense of humour.
MIKE	(*gasping*) Yeah.

LOUIS (*rising*) Well, we see ya, Eddie.

EDDIE Take it easy.

LOUIS Yeah. See ya.

MIKE If you wanna come bowlin' later we're goin' Flatbush Avenue.

Laughing, they move to exit, meeting RODOLFO *and* CATHERINE *entering on the street. Their laughter rises as they see* RODOLFO, *who does not understand but joins in.* EDDIE *moves to enter the house as* LOUIS *and* MIKE *exit.* CATHERINE *stops him at the door.*

CATHERINE Hey, Eddie – what a picture we saw! Did we laugh!

EDDIE (*he can't help smiling at sight of her*) Where'd you go?

CATHERINE Paramount. It was with those two guys, y'know? That –

EDDIE Brooklyn Paramount?

CATHERINE (*with an edge of anger, embarrassed before* RODOLFO) Sure, the Brooklyn Paramount. I told you we wasn't goin' to New York.

EDDIE (*retreating before the threat of her anger*) All right, I only asked you. (*To* RODOLFO) I just don't want her hangin' around Times Square, see? It's full of tramps over there.

RODOLFO I would like to go to Broadway once, Eddie. I would like to walk with her once where the theatres are and the opera. Since I was a boy I see pictures of those lights.

EDDIE (*his little patience waning*) I want to talk to her a minute, Rodolfo. Go inside, will you?

RODOLFO Eddie, we only walk together in the streets. She teaches me.

CATHERINE You know what he can't get over? That there's no fountains in Brooklyn!

EDDIE (*smiling unwillingly*) Fountains? (RODOLFO *smiles at his own naïveté.*)

CATHERINE In Italy he says, every town's got fountains, and they meet there. And you know what? They got oranges on the trees where he comes from, and lemons. Imagine – on the trees? I mean it's interesting. But he's crazy for New York.

RODOLFO (*attempting familiarity*) Eddie, why can't we go once to Broadway –?

EDDIE Look, I gotta tell her something –

RODOLFO Maybe you can come too. I want to see all those lights. (*He sees no response in* EDDIE *'s face. He glances at* CATHERINE.) I'll walk by the river before I go to sleep. (*He walks off down the street.*)

CATHERINE Why don't you talk to him, Eddie? He blesses you, and you don't talk to him hardly.

EDDIE (*enveloping her with his eyes*) I bless you and you don't talk to me. (*He tries to smile.*)

CATHERINE *I* don't talk to you? (*She hits his arm.*) What do you mean?

EDDIE I don't see you no more. I come home you're runnin' around someplace –

CATHERINE Well, he wants to see everything, that's all, so we go. ... You mad at me?

EDDIE No. (*He moves from her, smiling sadly.*) It's just I used to come home, you was always there. Now, I turn around, you're a big girl. I don't know how to talk to you.

CATHERINE Why?

EDDIE I don't know, you're runnin', you're runnin', Katie. I don't think you listening any more to me.

CATHERINE (*going to him*) Ah, Eddie, sure I am. What's the matter? You don't like him?

Slight pause.

EDDIE (*turns to her*) *You* like him, Katie?

CATHERINE (*with a blush but holding her ground*) Yeah. I like him.

EDDIE (*his smile goes*) You like him.

CATHERINE (*looking down*) Yeah. (*Now she looks at him for the consequences, smiling but tense. He looks at her like a lost boy.*) What're you got against him? I don't understand. He only blesses you.

EDDIE (*turns away*) He don't bless me, Katie.

CATHERINE He does! You're like a father to him!

EDDIE (*turns to her*) Katie.

CATHERINE What, Eddie?

EDDIE You gonna marry him?

CATHERINE I don't know. We just been ... goin' around, that's all. (*Turns to him*) What're you got against him, Eddie? Please, tell me. What?

EDDIE He don't respect you.

CATHERINE	Why?
EDDIE	Katie ... if you wasn't an orphan, wouldn't he ask your father's permission before he run around with you like this?
CATHERINE	Oh, well, he didn't think you'd mind.
EDDIE	He knows I mind, but it don't bother him if I mind, don't you see that?
CATHERINE	No, Eddie, he's got all kinds of respect for me. And you too! We walk across the street he takes my arm – he almost bows to me! You got him all wrong, Eddie; I mean it, you –
EDDIE	Katie, he's only bowin' to his passport.
CATHERINE	His passport?
EDDIE	That's right. He marries you he's got the right to be an American citizen. That's what's goin' on here. (*She is puzzled and surprised.*) You understand what I'm tellin' you? The guy is lookin' for his break, that's all he's lookin' for.
CATHERINE	(*pained*) Oh, no, Eddie, I don't think so.
EDDIE	You don't think so! Katie, you're gonna make me cry here. Is that a workin' man? What does he do with his first money? A snappy new jacket he buys, records, a pointy pair new shoes and his brother's kids are starvin' over there with tuberculosis? That's a hit-and-run guy, baby; he's got bright lights in his head, Broadway. Them guys don't think of nobody but theirself! You marry him and the next time you see him it'll be for divorce!
CATHERINE	(*steps toward him*) Eddie, he never said a word about his papers or –
EDDIE	You mean he's supposed to tell you that?
CATHERINE	I don't think he's even thinking about it.
EDDIE	What's better for him to think about! He could be picked up any day here and he's back pushin' taxis up the hill!
CATHERINE	No, I don't believe it.
EDDIE	Katie, don't break my heart, listen to me.
CATHERINE	I don't want to hear it.
EDDIE	Katie, listen ...
CATHERINE	He loves me!
EDDIE	(*with deep alarm*) Don't say that, for God's sake! This is the oldest racket in the country –
CATHERINE	(*desperately, as though he had made his imprint*) I don't believe it! (*She rushes to the house.*)

EDDIE   (*following her*) They been pullin' this since the Immigration Law was put in! They grab a green kid that don't know nothin' and they –

CATHERINE   (*sobbing*) I don't believe it and I wish to hell you'd stop it!

EDDIE   Katie!

They enter the apartment. The lights in the living room have risen and BEATRICE *is there. She looks past the sobbing* CATHERINE *at* EDDIE *who, in the presence of his wife, makes an awkward gesture of eroded command, indicating* CATHERINE.

EDDIE   Why don't you straighten her out?

BEATRICE   (*inwardly angered at his flowing emotion, which in itself alarms her*) When are you going to leave her alone?

EDDIE   B., the guy is no good!

BEATRICE   (*suddenly, with open fright and fury*) You going to leave her alone? Or you gonna drive me crazy? (*He turns, striving to retain his dignity, but nevertheless in guilt walks out of the house, into the street and away.* CATHERINE *starts into a bedroom.*) Listen, Catherine. (CATHERINE *halts, turns to her sheepishly.*) What are you going to do with yourself?

CATHERINE   I don't know.

BEATRICE   Don't tell me you don't know; you're not a baby any more, what are you going to do with yourself?

CATHERINE   He won't listen to me.

BEATRICE   I don't understand this. He's not your father, Catherine. I don't understand what's going on here.

CATHERINE   (*as one who herself is trying to rationalize a buried impulse*) What am I going to do, just kick him in the face with it?

BEATRICE   Look, honey, you wanna get married, or don't you wanna get married? What are you worried about, Katie?

CATHERINE   (*quietly, trembling*) I don't know B. It just seems wrong if he's against it so much.

BEATRICE   (*never losing her aroused alarm*) Sit down, honey, I want to tell you something. Here, sit down. Was there ever any fella he liked for you? There wasn't, was there?

CATHERINE   But he says Rodolfo's just after his papers.

BEATRICE   Look, he'll say anything. What does he care what he says? If it was a prince came here for you it would be no different. You know that, don't you?

CATHERINE	Yeah, I guess.
BEATRICE	So what does that mean?
CATHERINE	(*slowly turns her head to* BEATRICE) What?
BEATRICE	It means you gotta be your own self more. You still think you're a little girl, honey. But nobody else can make up your mind for you any more, you understand? You gotta give him to understand that he can't give you orders no more.
CATHERINE	Yeah, but how am I going to do that? He thinks I'm a baby.
BEATRICE	Because *you* think you're a baby. I told you fifty times already, you can't act the way you act. You still walk around in front of him in your slip –
CATHERINE	Well I forgot.
BEATRICE	Well you can't do it. Or like you sit on the edge of the bathtub talkin' to him when he's shavin' in his underwear.
CATHERINE	When'd I do that?
BEATRICE	I seen you in there this morning.
CATHERINE	Oh … well, I wanted to tell him something and I –
BEATRICE	I know, honey. But if you act like a baby and he be treatin' you like a baby. Like when he comes home sometimes you throw yourself at him like when you was twelve years old.
CATHERINE	Well I like to see him and I'm happy so I –
BEATRICE	Look, I'm not tellin' you what to do honey, but –
CATHERINE	No, you could tell me, B.! Gee, I'm all mixed up. See, I – He looks so sad now and it hurts me.
BEATRICE	Well look Katie, if it's goin' to hurt you so much you're gonna end up an old maid here.
CATHERINE	No!
BEATRICE	I'm tellin' you, I'm not makin' a joke. I tried to tell you a couple of times in the last year or so. That's why I was so happy you were going to go out and get work, you wouldn't be here so much, you'd be a little more independent. I mean it. It's wonderful for a whole family to love each other, but you're a grown woman and you're in the same house with a grown man. So you'll act different now, heh?
CATHERINE	Yeah, I will. I'll remember.
BEATRICE	Because it ain't only up to him, Katie, you understand? I told him the same thing already.
CATHERINE	(*quickly*) What?

BEATRICE   That he should let you go. But, you see, if only I tell him,
           he thinks I'm just bawlin' him out, or maybe I'm jealous or
           somethin', you know?

CATHERINE (*astonished*) He said you was jealous?

BEATRICE   No, I'm just sayin' maybe that's what he thinks. (*She
           reaches over to* CATHERINE'*s hand; with a strained smile*) You
           think I'm jealous of you, honey?

CATHERINE No! It's the first I thought of it.

BEATRICE   (*with a quiet sad laugh*) Well you should have thought of it
           before … but I'm not. We'll be all right. Just give him to
           understand; you don't have to fight, you're just – You're a
           woman, that's all, and you got a nice boy, and now the
           time came when you said good-bye. All right?

CATHERINE (*strangely moved at the prospect*) All right … If I can.

BEATRICE   Honey … you gotta.

           CATHERINE, *sensing now an imperious demand, turns with
           some fear, with a discovery, to* BEATRICE. *She is at the edge of
           tears, as though a familiar world had shattered.*

CATHERINE Okay.

           Lights out on them and up on ALFIERI, *seated behind his desk.*

ALFIERI   It was at this time that he first came to me. I had
           represented his father in an accident case some years
           before, and I was acquainted with the family in a casual
           way. I remember him now as he walked through my
           doorway –

           Enter EDDIE *down right ramp.*

           His eyes were like tunnels; my first thought was that he
           had committed a crime,

           EDDIE *sits beside the desk, cap in hand, looking out.*

           but soon I saw it was only a passion that had moved into
           his body, like a stranger. (ALFIERI *pauses, looks down at his
           desk, then to* EDDIE *as though he were continuing a
           conversation with him.*) I don't quite understand what I can
           do for you. Is there a question of law somewhere?

EDDIE   That's what I want to ask you.

ALFIERI   Because there's nothing illegal about a girl falling in love
           with an immigrant.

EDDIE   Yeah, but what about it if the only reason for it is to get his
           papers?

ALFIERI First of all you don't know that.

EDDIE I see it in his eyes; he's laughin' at her and he's laughin' at me.

ALFIERI Eddie, I'm a lawyer. I can only deal in what's provable. You understand that, don't you? Can you prove that?

EDDIE *I know what's in his mind, Mr Alfieri!*

ALFIERI Eddie, even if you could prove that –

EDDIE Listen … will you listen to me a minute? My father always said you was a smart man. I want you to listen to me.

ALFIERI I'm only a lawyer, Eddie.

EDDIE Will you listen a minute? I'm talkin' about the law. Lemme just bring out what I mean. A man, which he comes into the country illegal, don't it stand to reason he's gonna take every penny and put it in the sock? Because they don't know from one day to another, right?

ALFIERI All right.

EDDIE He's spendin'. Records he buys now. Shoes. Jackets. Y'understand me? This guy ain't worried. This guy is *here*. So it must be that he's got it all laid out in his mind already – he's stayin'. Right?

ALFIERI Well? What about it?

EDDIE All right. (*He glances at* ALFIERI, *then down to the floor.*) I'm talking to you confidential, ain't I?

ALFIERI Certainly.

EDDIE I mean it don't go no place but here. Because I don't like to say this about anybody. Even my wife I didn't exactly say this.

ALFIERI What is it?

EDDIE (*takes a breath and glances briefly over each shoulder*) The guy ain't right, Mr Alfieri.

ALFIERI What do you mean?

EDDIE I mean he ain't right.

ALFIERI I don't get you.

EDDIE (*shifts to another position in the chair*) Dja ever get a look at him?

ALFIERI Not that I know of, no.

EDDIE He's a blond guy. Like … platinum. You know what I mean?

ALFIERI No.

EDDIE	I mean if you close the paper fast – you could blow him over.
ALFIERI	Well that doesn't mean –
EDDIE	Wait a minute, I'm tellin' you sump'm. He sings, see. Which is – I mean it's all right, but sometimes he hits a note, see. I turn around. I mean – high. You know what I mean?
ALFIERI	Well, that's a tenor.
EDDIE	I know a tenor, Mr Alfieri. This ain't no tenor. I mean if you came in the house and you didn't know who was singin', you wouldn't be lookin' for him you be lookin' for her.
ALFIERI	Yes, but that's not –
EDDIE	I'm tellin' you sump'm, wait a minute. Please, Mr Alfieri. I'm tryin' to bring out my thoughts here. Couple of nights ago my niece brings out a dress which it's too small for her, because she shot up like a light this last year. He takes the dress, lays it on the table, he cuts it up; one-two-three, he makes a new dress. I mean he looked so sweet there, like an angel – you could kiss him he was so sweet.
ALFIERI	Now look, Eddie –
EDDIE	Mr Alfieri, they're laughin' at him on the piers. I'm ashamed. Paper Doll they call him. Blondie now. His brother thinks it's because he's got a sense of humour, see – which he's got – but that ain't what they're laughin'. Which they're not goin' to come out with it because they know he's my relative, which they have to see me if they make a crack, y'know? But I know what they're laughin' at, and when I think of that guy layin' his hands on her I could – I mean it's eatin' me out, Mr Alfieri, because I struggled for that girl. And now he comes in my house and –
ALFIERI	Eddie, look – I have my own children. I understand you. But the law is very specific. The law does not …
EDDIE	(*with a fuller flow of indignation*) You mean to tell me that there's no law that a guy which he ain't right can go to work and marry a girl and –?
ALFIERI	You have no recourse in the law, Eddie.
EDDIE	Yeah, but if he ain't right, Mr Alfieri, you mean to tell me –
ALFIERI	There is nothing you can do, Eddie, believe me.
EDDIE	Nothin'.

ALFIERI Nothing at all. There's only one legal question here.

EDDIE What?

ALFIERI The manner in which they entered the country. But I don't think you want to do anything about that, do you?

EDDIE You mean –?

ALFIERI Well, they entered illegally.

EDDIE Oh, Jesus, no, I wouldn't do nothin' about that, I mean –

ALFIERI All right, then, let me talk now, eh?

EDDIE Mr Alfieri, I can't believe what you tell me. I mean there must be some kinda law which –

ALFIERI Eddie, I want you to listen to me. (*Pause*) You know, sometimes God mixes up the people. We all love somebody, the wife, the kids – every man's got somebody that he loves, heh? But sometimes ... there's too much. You know? There's too much, and it goes where it mustn't. A man works hard, he brings up a child, sometimes it's a niece, sometimes even a daughter, and he never realizes it, but through the years – there is too much love for the daughter, there is too much love for the niece. Do you understand what I'm saying to you?

EDDIE (*sardonically*) What do you mean, I shouldn't look out for her good?

ALFIERI Yes, but these things have to end, Eddie, that's all. The child has to grow up and go away, and the man has to learn to forget. Because after all, Eddie – what other way can it end? (*Pause*) Let her go. That's my advice. You did your job, now it's her life; wish her luck, and let her go. (*Pause*) Will you do that? Because there's no law, Eddie; make up your mind to it; the law is not interested in this.

EDDIE You mean to tell me, even if he's a punk? If he's –

ALFIERI There's nothing you can do.

EDDIE *stands*.

EDDIE Well, all right, thanks. Thanks very much.

ALFIERI What are you going to do?

EDDIE (*with a helpless but ironic gesture*) What can I do? I'm a patsy, what can a patsy do? I worked like a dog twenty years so a punk could have her, so that's what I done. I mean, in the worst times, in the worst, when there wasn't a ship comin' in the harbour, I didn't stand around lookin' for relief – I hustled. When there was empty piers in Brooklyn I went to Hoboken, Staten

Island, the West Side, Jersey, all over – because I made a
promise. I took out of my own mouth to give to her. I took
out of my wife's mouth. I walked hungry plenty days in
this city! (*It begins to break through.*) And now I gotta sit in
my own house and look at a son-of-a-bitch punk like that
– which he came out of nowhere! I give him my house to
sleep! I take the blankets off my bed for him, and he takes
and puts his filthy hands on her like a goddam thief!

ALFIERI   (*rising*) But, Eddie, she's a woman now.

EDDIE   He's stealing from me!

ALFIERI   She wants to get married, Eddie. She can't marry you, can
she?

EDDIE   (*furiously*) What're you talkin' about, marry me! I don't
know what the hell you're talkin' about!
Pause.

ALFIERI   I gave you my advice, Eddie. That's it.
EDDIE *gathers himself. A pause.*

EDDIE   Well, thanks. Thanks very much. It just – it's breakin' my
heart, y'know. I –

ALFIERI   I understand. Put it out of your mind. Can you do that?

EDDIE   I'm – (*He feels the threat of sobs, and with a helpless wave.*)
I'll see you around. (*He goes out up the right ramp.*)

ALFIERI   (*sits on desk*) There are times when you want to spread an
alarm, but nothing has happened. I knew, I knew then and
there – I could have finished the whole story that
afternoon. It wasn't as though there was a mystery to
unravel. I could see every step coming, step after step, like
a dark figure walking down a hall toward a certain door. I
knew where he was heading for, I knew where he was
going to end. And I sat here many afternoons asking
myself why, being an intelligent man, I was so powerless
to stop it. I even went to a certain old lady in the
neighbourhood, a very wise old woman, and I told her,
and she only nodded, and said, 'Pray for him ...' And so I
– waited here.
As lights go out on ALFIERI, *they rise in the apartment where
all are finishing dinner.* BEATRICE *and* CATHERINE *are clearing
the table.*

CATHERINE   You know where they went?

BEATRICE   Where?

CATHERINE	They went to Africa once. On a fishing boat. (EDDIE *glances at her.*) It's true, Eddie.
	BEATRICE *exits into the kitchen with dishes.*
EDDIE	I didn't say nothin'. (*He goes to his rocker, picks up a newspaper.*)
CATHERINE	And I was never even in Staten Island.
EDDIE	(*sitting with the paper*) You didn't miss nothin'. (*Pause.* CATHERINE *takes dishes out.*) How long that take you, Marco – to get to Africa?
MARCO	(*rising*) Oh ... two days. We go all over.
RODOLFO	(*rising*) Once we went to Yugoslavia.
EDDIE	(*to* MARCO) They pay all right on them boats?
	BEATRICE *enters. She and* RODOLFO *stack the remaining dishes.*
MARCO	If they catch fish they pay all right. (*Sits on a stool.*)
RODOLFO	They're family boats, though. And nobody in our family owned one. So we only worked when one of the families was sick.
BEATRICE	Y'know, Marco, what I don't understand – there's an ocean full of fish and yiz are all starvin'.
EDDIE	They gotta have boats, nets, you need money.
	CATHERINE *enters.*
BEATRICE	Yeah, but couldn't they like fish from the beach? You see them down Coney Island –
MARCO	Sardines.
EDDIE	Sure. (*laughing*) How you gonna catch sardines on a hook?
BEATRICE	Oh, I didn't know they're sardines. (*To* CATHERINE) They're sardines!
CATHERINE	Yeah, they follow them all over the ocean, Africa, Yugoslavia ... (*She sits and begins to look through a movie magazine.* RODOLFO *joins her.*)
BEATRICE	(*to* EDDIE) It's funny, y'know. You never think of it, that sardines are swimming in the ocean! (*She exits to kitchen with dishes.*)
CATHERINE	I know. It's like oranges and lemons on a tree. (*To* EDDIE) I mean you ever think of oranges and lemons on a tree?
EDDIE	Yeah, I know. It's funny. (*To* MARCO) I heard that they paint the oranges to make them look orange.
	BEATRICE *enters.*

MARCO	(*he has been reading a letter*) Paint?
EDDIE	Yeah, I heard that they grow like green.
MARCO	No, in Italy the oranges are orange.
RODOLFO	Lemons are green.
EDDIE	(*resenting his instruction*) I know lemons are green, for Christ's sake, you see them in the store they're green sometimes. I said oranges they paint, I didn't say nothin' about lemons.
BEATRICE	(*sitting; diverting their attention*) Your wife is gettin' the money all right, Marco?
MARCO	Oh, yes. She bought medicine for my boy.
BEATRICE	That's wonderful. You feel better, heh?
MARCO	Oh, yes! But I'm lonesome.
BEATRICE	I just hope you ain't gonna do like some of them around here. They're here twenty-five years, some men, and they didn't get enough together to go back twice.
MARCO	Oh, I know. We have many families in our town, the children never saw the father. But I will go home. Three, four years, I think.
BEATRICE	Maybe you should keep more here. Because maybe she thinks it comes so easy you'll never get ahead of yourself.
MARCO	Oh, no, she saves. I send everything. My wife is very lonesome. (*He smiles shyly.*)
BEATRICE	She must be nice. She pretty? I bet, heh?
MARCO	(*blushing*) No, but she understand everything.
RODOLFO	Oh, he's got a clever wife!
EDDIE	I betcha there's plenty surprises sometimes when those guys get back there, heh?
MARCO	Surprises?
EDDIE	(*laughing*) I mean, you know – they count the kids and there's a couple extra than when they left?
MARCO	No – no … The women wait, Eddie. Most. Most. Very few surprises.
RODOLFO	It's more strict in our town. (EDDIE *looks at him now.*) It's not so free.
EDDIE	(*rises, paces up and down*) It ain't so free here either, Rodolfo, like you think. I seen greenhorns sometimes get in trouble that way – they think just because a girl don't go around with a shawl over her head that she ain't strict, y'know? Girl don't have to wear black dress to be strict. Know what I mean?

RODOLFO Well, I always have respect –

EDDIE I know, but in your town you wouldn't just drag off some girl without permission, I mean. (*He turns.*) You know what I mean, Marco? It ain't that much different here.

MARCO (*cautiously*) Yes.

BEATRICE Well, he didn't exactly drag her off though, Eddie.

EDDIE I know, but I seen some of them get the wrong idea sometimes. (*To* RODOLFO) I mean it might be a little more free here but it's just as strict.

RODOLFO I have respect for her, Eddie. I do anything wrong?

EDDIE Look, kid, I ain't her father, I'm only her uncle –

BEATRICE Well then, be an uncle then. (EDDIE *looks at her, aware of her criticizing force.*) I *mean.*

MARCO No, Beatrice, if he does wrong you must tell him. (*To* EDDIE) What does he do wrong?

EDDIE Well, Marco, till he came here she was never out on the street twelve o'clock at night.

MARCO (*to* RODOLFO) You come home early now.

BEATRICE (*to* CATHERINE) Well, you said the movie ended late, didn't you?

CATHERINE Yeah.

BEATRICE Well, tell him, honey. (*To* EDDIE) The movie ended late.

EDDIE Look, B., I'm just sayin' – he thinks she always stayed out like that.

MARCO You come home early now, Rodolfo.

RODOLFO (*embarrassed*) All right, sure. But I can't stay in the house all the time, Eddie.

EDDIE Look, kid, I'm not only talkin' about her. The more you run around like that the more chance you're takin'. (*To* BEATRICE) I mean suppose he gets hit by a car or something. (*To* MARCO) Where's his papers, who is he? Know what I mean?

BEATRICE Yeah, but who is he in the daytime, though? It's the same chance in the daytime.

EDDIE (*holding back a voice full of anger*) Yeah, but he don't have to go lookin' for it, Beatrice. If he's here to work, then he should work; if he's here for a good time then he could fool around! (*To* MARCO) But I understood, Marco, that you was both comin' to make a livin' for your family. You understand me, don't you, Marco? (*He goes to his rocker.*)

MARCO	I beg your pardon, Eddie.
EDDIE	I mean, that's what I understood in the first place, see.
MARCO	Yes. That's why we came.
EDDIE	(*sits on his rocker*) Well, that's all I'm askin'.

EDDIE *reads his paper. There is a pause, an awkwardness. Now* CATHERINE *gets up and puts a record on the phonograph – 'Paper Doll'.*

CATHERINE	(*flushed with revolt*) You wanna dance, Rodolfo? (EDDIE *freezes.*)
RODOLFO	(*in deference to* EDDIE) No, I – I'm tired.
BEATRICE	Go ahead, dance, Rodolfo.
CATHERINE	Ah, come on. They got a beautiful quartet, these guys. Come.

She has taken his hand and he stiffly rises, feeling EDDIE*'s eyes on his back, and they dance.*

EDDIE	(*to* CATHERINE) What's that, a new record?
CATHERINE	It's the same one. We bought it the other day.
BEATRICE	(*to* EDDIE) They only bought three records. (*She watches them dance;* EDDIE *turns his head away.* MARCO *just sits there waiting. Now* BEATRICE *turns to* EDDIE.) Must be nice to go all over in one of them fishin' boats. I would like that myself. See all them other countries?
EDDIE	Yeah.
BEATRICE	(*to* MARCO) But the women don't go along, I bet.
MARCO	No, not on the boats. Hard work.
BEATRICE	What're you got, a regular kitchen and everything?
MARCO	Yes, we eat very good on the boats – especially when Rodolfo comes along; everybody gets fat.
BEATRICE	Oh, he cooks?
MARCO	Sure, very good cook. Rice, pasta, fish, everything.

EDDIE *lowers his newspaper.*

EDDIE	He's a cook, too! (*Looking at* RODOLFO) He sings, he cooks …

RODOLFO *smiles thankfully.*

BEATRICE	Well it's good, he could always make a living.
EDDIE	It's wonderful. He sings, he cooks, he could make dresses …
CATHERINE	They get some high pay, them guys. The head chefs in all the big hotels are men. You read about them.

EDDIE That's what I'm sayin'.

CATHERINE *and* RODOLFO *continue dancing.*

CATHERINE Yeah, well, I mean.

EDDIE (*to* BEATRICE) He's lucky, believe me. (*Slight pause. He looks away, then back to* BEATRICE.) That's why the water front is no place for him. (*They stop dancing.* RODOLFO *turns off phonograph.*) I mean like me – I can't cook, I can't sing, I can't make dresses, so I'm on the water front. But if I could cook, if I could sing, if I could make dresses, I wouldn't be on the water front. (*He has been unconsciously twisting the newspaper into a tight roll. They are all regarding him now; he senses he is exposing the issue and he is driven on.*) I would be someplace else. I would be like in a dress store. (*He has bent the rolled paper and it suddenly tears in two. He suddenly gets up and pulls his pants up over his belly and goes to* MARCO.) What do you say, Marco, we go to the bouts next Saturday night. You never seen a fight, did you?

MARCO (*uneasy*) Only in the moving pictures.

EDDIE (*goes to* RODOLFO) I'll treat yiz. What do you say, Danish? You wanna come along? I'll buy the tickets.

RODOLFO Sure. I like to go.

CATHERINE (*going to* EDDIE; *nervously happy now*) I'll make some coffee, all right?

EDDIE Go ahead, make some! Make it nice and strong. (*Mystified, she smiles and exits to kitchen. He is weirdly elated, rubbing his fists into his palms. He strides to* MARCO) You wait, Marco, you see some real fights here. You ever do any boxing?

MARCO No, I never.

EDDIE (*to* RODOLFO) Betcha you have done some, heh?

RODOLFO No.

EDDIE Well, come on, I'll teach you.

BEATRICE What's he got to learn that for?

EDDIE Ya can't tell, one of these days somebody's liable to step on his foot or sump'm. Come on, Rodolfo, I show you a couple a passes. (*He stands below table.*)

BEATRICE Go ahead, Rodolfo. He's a good boxer, he could teach you.

RODOLFO (*embarrassed*) Well, I don't know how to – (*He moves down to* EDDIE.)

EDDIE Just put your hands up. Like this, see? That's right. That's very good, keep your left up, because you lead with the left, see, like this. (*He gently moves his left into* RODOLFO*'s face.*) See? Now what you gotta do is you gotta block me, so when I come in like that you – (RODOLFO *parries his left.*) Hey, that's very good! (RODOLFO *laughs.*) All right, now come into me. Come on.

RODOLFO   I don't want to hit you, Eddie.

EDDIE   Don't pity me, come on. Throw it, I'll show you how to block it. (RODOLFO *jabs at him, laughing. The others join.*) 'At's it. Come on again. For the jaw right here. (RODOLFO *jabs with more assurance.*) Very good!

BEATRICE   (*to* MARCO) He's very good!

EDDIE *crosses directly upstage of* RODOLFO.

EDDIE   Sure, he's great! Come on, kid, put sump'm behind it, you can't hurt me. (RODOLFO*, more seriously, jabs at* EDDIE*'s jaw and grazes it.*) Attaboy.

CATHERINE *comes from the kitchen, watches.*

Now I'm gonna hit you, so block me, see?

CATHERINE   (*with beginning alarm*) What are they doin'?

They are lightly boxing now.

BEATRICE   (*she senses only the comradeship in it now*) He's teachin' him; he's very good!

EDDIE   Sure, he's terrific! Look at him go! (RODOLFO *lands a blow.*) 'At's it! Now, watch out, here I come, Danish! (*He feints with his left hand and lands with his right. It mildly staggers* RODOLFO. MARCO *rises.*)

CATHERINE   (*rushing to* RODOLFO) Eddie!

EDDIE   Why? I didn't hurt him. Did I hurt you, kid? (*He rubs the back of his hand across his mouth.*)

RODOLFO   No, no, he didn't hurt me. (*To* EDDIE *with a certain gleam and a smile*) I was only surprised.

BEATRICE   (*pulling* EDDIE *down into the rocker*) That's enough, Eddie; he did pretty good though.

EDDIE   Yeah. (*Rubbing his fists together*) He could be very good, Marco. I'll teach him again.

MARCO *nods at him dubiously.*

RODOLFO   Dance, Catherine. Come. (*He takes her hand; they go to phonograph and start it. It plays 'Paper Doll'.*

RODOLFO *takes her in his arms. They dance.* EDDIE *in thought*

> *sits in his chair, and* MARCO *takes a chair, places it in front of* EDDIE, *and looks down at it.* BEATRICE *and* EDDIE *watch him.*

MARCO Can you lift this chair?

EDDIE What do you mean?

MARCO From here. (*He gets on one knee with one hand behind his back, and grasps the bottom of one of the chair legs but does not raise it.*)

EDDIE Sure, why not? (*He comes to the chair, kneels, grasps the leg, raises the chair one inch, but it leans over to the floor.*) Gee, that's hard, I never knew that. (*He tries again, and again fails.*) It's on an angle, that's why, heh?

MARCO Here. (*He kneels, grasps, and with strain slowly raises the chair higher and higher, getting to his feet now.* RODOLFO *and* CATHERINE *have stopped dancing as* MARCO *raises the chair over his head.*

> MARCO *is face to face with* EDDIE, *a strained tension gripping his eyes and jaw, his neck stiff, the chair raised like a weapon over* EDDIE's *head – and he transforms what might appear like a glare of warning into a smile of triumph, and* EDDIE's *grin vanishes as he absorbs his look.*

CURTAIN

ACT TWO

Light rises on ALFIERI *at his desk.*

ALFIERI On the twenty-third of that December a case of Scotch whisky slipped from a net while being unloaded – as a case of Scotch whisky is inclined to do on the twenty-third of December on Pier Forty-one. There was no snow, but it was cold, his wife was out shopping. Marco was still at work. The boy had not been hired that day; Catherine told me later that this was the first time they had been alone together in the house.

Light is rising on CATHERINE *in the apartment.* RODOLFO *is watching as she arranges a paper pattern on cloth spread on the table.*

CATHERINE You hungry?

RODOLFO Not for anything to eat. (*Pause*) I have nearly three hundred dollars. Catherine?

CATHERINE I heard you.

RODOLFO You don't like to talk about it any more?

CATHERINE Sure, I don't mind talkin' about it.

RODOLFO What worries you, Catherine?

CATHERINE I been wantin' to ask you about something. Could I?

RODOLFO All the answers are in my eyes, Catherine. But you don't look in my eyes lately. You're full of secrets. (*She looks at him. She seems withdrawn.*) What is the question?

CATHERINE Suppose I wanted to live in Italy.

RODOLFO (*smiling at the incongruity*) You going to marry somebody rich?

CATHERINE No, I mean live there – you and me.

RODOLFO (*his smile vanishing*) When?

CATHERINE Well ... when we get married.

RODOLFO   (*astonished.*) You want to be an Italian?

CATHERINE   No, but I could live there without being Italian. Americans live there.

RODOLFO   Forever?

CATHERINE   Yeah.

RODOLFO   (*crosses to rocker*) You're fooling.

CATHERINE   No, I mean it.

RODOLFO   Where do you get such an idea?

CATHERINE   Well, you're always saying it's so beautiful there, with the mountains and the ocean and all the –

RODOLFO   You're fooling me.

CATHERINE   I mean it.

RODOLFO   (*goes to her slowly*) Catherine, if I ever brought you home with no money, no business, nothing, they would call the priest and the doctor and they would say Rodolfo is crazy.

CATHERINE   I know, but I think we would be happier there.

RODOLFO   Happier! What would you eat? You can't cook the view!

CATHERINE   Maybe you could be a singer, like in Rome or –

RODOLFO   Rome! Rome is full of singers.

CATHERINE   Well, I could work then.

RODOLFO   Where?

CATHERINE   God, there must be jobs somewhere!

RODOLFO   There's nothing! Nothing, nothing, nothing. Now tell me what you're talking about. How can I bring you from a rich country to suffer in a poor country? What are you talking about? (*She searches for words.*) I would be a criminal stealing your face. In two years you would have an old, hungry face. When my brother's babies cry they give them water, water that boiled a bone. Don't you believe that?

CATHERINE   (*quietly*) I'm afraid of Eddie here.

     Slight pause.

RODOLFO   (*steps closer to her*) We wouldn't live here. Once I am a citizen I could work anywhere and I would find better jobs and we would have a house, Catherine. If I were not afraid to be arrested I would start to be something wonderful here!

CATHERINE   (*steeling herself*) Tell me something. I mean just tell me, Rodolfo – would you still want to do it if it turned out we had to go live in Italy? I mean just if it turned out that way.

RODOLFO	This is your question or his question?
CATHERINE	I would like to know, Rodolfo. I mean it.
RODOLFO	To go there with nothing.
CATHERINE	Yeah.
RODOLFO	No. (*She looks at him wide-eyed.*) No.
CATHERINE	You wouldn't?
RODOLFO	No; I will not marry you to live in Italy. I want you to be my wife, and I want to be a citizen. Tell him that, or I will. Yes. (*He moves about angrily.*) And tell him also, and tell yourself, please, that I am not a beggar, and you are not a horse, a gift, a favour for a poor immigrant.
CATHERINE	Well, don't get mad!
RODOLFO	I am furious! (*Goes to her.*) Do you think I am so desperate? My brother is desperate, not me. You think I would carry on my back the rest of my life a woman I didn't love just to be an American? It's so wonderful? You think we have no tall buildings in Italy? Electric lights? No wide streets? No flags? No automobiles? Only work we don't have. I want to be an American so I can work, that is the only wonder here – work! How can you insult me, Catherine?
CATHERINE	I didn't mean that –
RODOLFO	My heart dies to look at you. Why are you so afraid of him?
CATHERINE	(*near tears*) I don't know!
RODOLFO	Do you trust me, Catherine? You?
CATHERINE	It's only that I – He was good to me, Rodolfo. You don't know him; he was always the sweetest guy to me. Good. He razzes me all the time but he don't mean it. I know. I would – just feel ashamed if I made him sad. 'Cause I always dreamt that when I got married he would be happy at the wedding, and laughin' – and now he's – mad all the time and nasty – (*She is weeping.*) Tell him you'd live in Italy – just tell him, and maybe he would start to trust you a little, see? Because I want him to be happy; I mean – I like him, Rodolfo – and I can't stand it!
RODOLFO	Oh, Catherine – oh, little girl.
CATHERINE	I love you, Rodolfo, I love you.
RODOLFO	Then why are you afraid? That he'll spank you?
CATHERINE	Don't, don't laugh at me! I've been here all my life. … Every day I saw him when he left in the morning and when

he came home at night. You think it's so easy to turn around and say to a man he's nothin' to you no more?

RODOLFO   I know, but –

CATHERINE   You don't know; nobody knows! I'm not a baby, I know a lot more than people think I know. Beatrice says to be a woman, but –

RODOLFO   Yes.

CATHERINE   Then why don't she be a woman? If I was a wife I would make a man happy instead of goin' at him all the time. I can tell a block away when he's blue in his mind and just wants to talk to somebody quiet and nice ... I can tell when he's hungry or wants a beer before he even says anything. I know when his feet hurt him, I mean I *know* him and now I'm supposed to turn around and make a stranger out of him? I don't know why I have to do that, I mean.

RODOLFO   Catherine. If I take in my hands a little bird. And she grows and wishes to fly. But I will not let her out of my hands because I love her so much, is that right for me to do? I don't say you must hate him; but anyway you must go, mustn't you? Catherine?

CATHERINE   (*softly*) Hold me.

RODOLFO   (*clasping her to him*) Oh, my little girl.

CATHERINE   Teach me. (*She is weeping.*) I don't know anything, teach me, Rodolfo, hold me.

RODOLFO   There's nobody here now. Come inside. Come. (*He is leading her toward the bedrooms.*) And don't cry any more.

Light rises on the street. In a moment EDDIE *appears. He is unsteady, drunk. He mounts the stairs. He enters the apartment, looks around, takes out a bottle from one pocket, puts it on the table. Then another bottle from another pocket, and a third from an inside pocket. He sees the pattern and cloth, goes over to it and touches it, and turns toward upstage.*

EDDIE   Beatrice? (*He goes to the open kitchen door and looks in.*) Beatrice? Beatrice?

CATHERINE *enters from bedroom; under his gaze she adjusts her dress.*

CATHERINE   You got home early.

EDDIE   Knocked off for Christmas early. (*Indicating the pattern*) Rodolfo makin' you a dress?

CATHERINE   No. I'm makin' a blouse.

                 RODOLFO *appears in the bedroom doorway.* EDDIE *sees him
                 and his arm jerks slightly in shock.* RODOLFO *nods to him
                 testingly.*

RODOLFO   Beatrice went to buy presents for her mother.

                 Pause.

EDDIE   Pack it up. Go ahead. Get your stuff and get outa here.
                 (CATHERINE *instantly turns and walks toward the bedroom,
                 and* EDDIE *grabs her arm.*) Where you goin'?

CATHERINE   (*trembling with fright*) I think I have to get out of here,
                 Eddie.

EDDIE   No, you ain't goin' nowheres, he's the one.

CATHERINE   I think I can't stay here no more. (*She frees her arm, steps
                 back toward the bedroom.*) I'm sorry, Eddie. (*She sees the
                 tears in his eyes.*) Well, don't cry. I'll be around the
                 neighbourhood; I'll see you. I just can't stay here no
                 more. You know I can't. (*Her sobs of pity and love for him
                 break her composure.*) Don't you know I can't? You know
                 that, don't you? (*She goes to him.*) Wish me luck. (*She
                 clasps her hands prayerfully.*) Oh, Eddie, don't be like
                 that!

EDDIE   You ain't goin' nowheres.

CATHERINE   Eddie, I'm not gonna be a baby any more! You –

                 *He reaches out suddenly, draws her to him, and as she
                 strives to free herself he kisses her on the mouth.*

RODOLFO   Don't! (*He pulls on* EDDIE*'s arm.*) Stop that! Have respect
                 for her!

EDDIE   (*spun round by* RODOLFO) You want something?

RODOLFO   Yes! She'll be my wife. That is what I want. My wife!

EDDIE   But what're you gonna be?

RODOLFO   I show you what I be!

CATHERINE   Wait outside; don't argue with him!

EDDIE   Come on, show me! What're you gonna be? Show me!

RODOLFO   (*with tears of rage*) Don't say that to me!

                 RODOLFO *flies at him in attack.* EDDIE *pins his arms,
                 laughing, and suddenly kisses him.*

CATHERINE   Eddie! Let go, ya hear me! I'll kill you! Leggo of him!

                 She tears at EDDIE*'s face and* EDDIE *releases* RODOLFO. EDDIE *stands there with tears rolling down his face as he laughs mockingly at* RODOLFO. *She is staring at him in horror.* RODOLFO *is rigid. They are like animals that have torn at one another and broken up without a decision, each waiting for the other's mood.*

EDDIE   (*to* CATHERINE) You see? (*To* RODOLFO) I give you till tomorrow, kid. Get outa here. Alone. You hear me? Alone.

CATHERINE   I'm going with him, Eddie. (*She starts toward* RODOLFO.)

EDDIE   (*indicating* RODOLFO *with his head*) Not with that. (*She halts, frightened. He sits, still panting for breath, and they watch him helplessly as he leans toward them over the table.*) Don't make me do nuttin', Catherine. Watch your step, submarine. By rights they oughta throw you back in the water. But I got pity for you. (*He moves uneasily toward the door, always facing* RODOLFO.) Just get outa here and don't lay another hand on her unless you wanna go out feet first. (*He goes out of the apartment.*)

The lights go down, as they rise on ALFIERI.

ALFIERI   On December twenty-seventh I saw him next. I normally go home well before six, but that day I sat around looking out my window at the bay, and when I saw him walking through my doorway, I knew why I had waited. And if I seem to tell this like a dream, it was that way. Several moments arrived in the course of the two talks we had when it occurred to me how – almost transfixed I had come to feel. I had lost my strength somewhere. (EDDIE *enters, removing his cap, sits in the chair, looks thoughtfully out.*) I looked in his eyes more than I listened – in fact, I can hardly remember the conversation. But I will never forget how dark the room became when he looked at me; his eyes were like tunnels. I kept wanting to call the police, but nothing had happened. Nothing at all had really happened. (*He breaks off and looks down at the desk. Then he turns to* EDDIE.) So in other words, he won't leave?

EDDIE   My wife is talkin' about renting a room upstairs for them. An old lady on the top floor is got an empty room.

ALFIERI   What does Marco say?

EDDIE   He just sits there. Marco don't say much.

ALFIERI   I guess they didn't tell him, heh? What happened?

EDDIE   I don't know; Marco don't say much.

ALFIERI   What does your wife say?

EDDIE   (*unwilling to pursue this*) Nobody's talkin' much in the
house. So what about that?

ALFIERI   But you didn't prove anything about him. It sounds like he
just wasn't strong enough to break your grip.

EDDIE   I'm tellin' you I know – he ain't right. Somebody that don't
want it can break it. Even a mouse, if you catch a teeny
mouse and you hold it in your hand, that mouse can give
you the right kind of fight. He didn't give me the right kind
of fight, I know it, Mr Alfieri, the guy ain't right.

ALFIERI   What did you do that for, Eddie?

EDDIE   To show her what he is! So she would see, once and for all!
Her mother'll turn over in the grave! (*He gathers himself
almost peremptorily.*) So what do I gotta do now? Tell me
what to do.

ALFIERI   She actually said she's marrying him?

EDDIE   She told me, yeah. So what do I do?

Slight pause.

ALFIERI   This is my last word, Eddie, take it or not, that's your
business. Morally and legally you have no rights, you
cannot stop it; she is a free agent.

EDDIE   (*angering*) Didn't you hear what I told you?

ALFIERI   (*with a tougher tone*) I heard what you told me, and I'm
telling you what the answer is. I'm not only telling you
now, I'm warning you – the law is nature. The law is only a
word for what has a right to happen. When the law is
wrong it's because it's unnatural, but in this case it is natural
and a river will drown you if you buck it now. Let her go.
And bless her. (*A phone booth begins to glow on the opposite
side of the stage; a faint, lonely blue.* EDDIE *stands up, jaws
clenched.*) Somebody had to come for her, Eddie, sooner or
later. (EDDIE *starts turning to go and* ALFIERI *rises with new
anxiety.*) You won't have a friend in the world, Eddie! Even
those who understand will turn against you, even the ones
who feel the same will despise you! (EDDIE *moves off.*) Put it
out of your mind! Eddie! (*He follows into the darkness,
calling desperately.*)

EDDIE *is gone. The phone is glowing in light now. Light is out
on* ALFIERI. EDDIE *has at the same time appeared beside the
phone.*

EDDIE	Give me the number of the Immigration Bureau. Thanks. (*He dials.*) I want to report something. Illegal immigrants. Two of them. That's right. Four-forty-one Saxon Street, Brooklyn, yeah. Ground floor. Heh? (*With greater difficulty*) I'm just around the neighbourhood, that's all. Heh? *Evidently he is being questioned further, and he slowly hangs up. He leaves the phone just as* LOUIS *and* MIKE *come down the street.*
LOUIS	Go bowlin', Eddie?
EDDIE	No, I'm due home.
LOUIS	Well, take it easy.
EDDIE	I'll see yiz.
	They leave him, exiting right, and he watches them go. He glances about, then goes up into the house. The lights go on in the apartment. BEATRICE *is taking down Christmas decorations and packing them in a box.*
EDDIE	Where is everybody? (BEATRICE *does not answer.*) I says where is everybody?
BEATRICE	(*looking up at him, wearied with it, and concealing a fear of him*) I decided to move them upstairs with Mrs Dondero.
EDDIE	Oh, they're all moved up there already?
BEATRICE	Yeah.
EDDIE	Where's Catherine? She up there?
BEATRICE	Only to bring pillow cases.
EDDIE	She ain't movin' in with them.
BEATRICE	Look, I'm sick and tired of it. I'm sick and tired of it!
EDDIE	All right, all right, take it easy.
BEATRICE	I don't wanna hear no more about it, you understand? Nothin'!
EDDIE	What're you blowin' off about? Who brought them in here?
BEATRICE	All right, I'm sorry; I wish I'd a drop dead before I told them to come. In the ground I wish I was.
EDDIE	Don't drop dead, just keep in mind who brought them in here, that's all. (*He moves about restlessly.*) I mean I got a couple of rights here. (*He moves, wanting to beat down her evident disapproval of him.*) This is my house here not their house.
BEATRICE	What do you want from me? They're moved out; what do you want now?
EDDIE	I want my respect!

BEATRICE	So I moved them out, what more do you want? You got your house now, you got your respect.
EDDIE	(*he moves about biting his lip*) I don't like the way you talk to me, Beatrice.
BEATRICE	I'm just tellin' you I done what you want!
EDDIE	I don't like it! The way you talk to me and the way you look at me. This is my house. And she is my niece and I'm responsible for her.
BEATRICE	So that's why you done that to him?
EDDIE	I done what to him?
BEATRICE	What you done to him in front of her; you know what I'm talkin' about. She goes around shakin' all the time, she can't go to sleep! That's what you call responsible for her?
EDDIE	(*quietly*) The guy ain't right, Beatrice. (*She is silent.*) Did you hear what I said?
BEATRICE	Look, I'm finished with it. That's all. (*She resumes her work.*)
EDDIE	(*helping her to pack the tinsel*) I'm gonna have it out with you one of these days, Beatrice.
BEATRICE	Nothin' to have out with me, it's all settled. Now we gonna be like it never happened, that's all.
EDDIE	I want my respect, Beatrice, and you know what I'm talkin' about.
BEATRICE	What?
	Pause.
EDDIE	(*finally his resolution hardens*) What I feel like doin' in the bed and what I don't feel like doin'. I don't want no –
BEATRICE	When'd I say anything about that?
EDDIE	You said, you said, I ain't deaf. I don't want no more conversations about that, Beatrice. I do what I feel like doin' or what I don't feel like doin'.
BEATRICE	Okay.
	Pause.
EDDIE	You used to be different, Beatrice. You had a whole different way.
BEATRICE	*I'm* no different.
EDDIE	You didn't used to jump me all the time about everything. The last year or two I come in the house I don't know what's gonna hit me. It's a shootin' gallery in here and I'm the pigeon.

BEATRICE	Okay, okay.
EDDIE	Don't tell me okay, okay, I'm tellin' you the truth. A wife is supposed to believe the husband. If I tell you that guy ain't right don't tell me he is right.
BEATRICE	But how do you know?
EDDIE	Because I know. I don't go around makin' accusations. He give me the heeby-jeebies the first minute I seen him. And I don't like you sayin' I don't want her marryin' anybody. I broke my back payin' her stenography lessons so she could go out and meet a better class of people. Would I do that if I didn't want her to get married? Sometimes you talk like I was a crazy man or sump'm.
BEATRICE	But she likes him.
EDDIE	Beatrice, she's a baby, how is she gonna know what she likes?
BEATRICE	Well, you kept her a baby, you wouldn't let her go out. I told you a hundred times.

Pause.

EDDIE	All right. Let her go out, then.
BEATRICE	She don't wanna go out now. It's too late, Eddie.

Pause.

EDDIE	Suppose I told her to go out. Suppose I –
BEATRICE	They're going to get married next week, Eddie.
EDDIE	(*his head jerks around to her*) She said that?
BEATRICE	Eddie, if you want my advice, go to her and tell her good luck. I think maybe now that you had it out you learned better.
EDDIE	What's the hurry next week?
BEATRICE	Well, she's been worried about him bein' picked up; this way he could start to be a citizen. She loves him, Eddie. (*He gets up, moves about uneasily, restlessly.*) Why don't you give her a good word? Because I still think she would like you to be a friend, y'know? (*He is standing, looking at the floor.*) I mean like if you told her you'd go to the wedding.
EDDIE	She asked you that?
BEATRICE	I know she would like it. I'd like to make a party here for her. I mean there oughta be some kinda send-off. Heh? I mean she'll have trouble enough in her life, let's start it off happy. What do you say? 'Cause in her heart she still loves you, Eddie. I know it. (*He presses his fingers against his eyes.*) What're you,

	cryin'? (*She goes to him, holds his face.*) Go ... whyn't you go tell her you're sorry? (CATHERINE *is seen on the upper landing of the stairway, and they hear her descending.*) There ... she's comin' down. Come on, shake hands with her.
EDDIE	(*moving with suppressed suddenness*) No, I can't, I can't talk to her.
BEATRICE	Eddie, give her a break; a wedding should be happy!
EDDIE	I'm goin', I'm goin' for a walk.
	He goes upstage for his jacket. CATHERINE *enters and starts for the bedroom door.*
BEATRICE	Katie? ... Eddie, don't go, wait a minute. (*She embraces* EDDIE*'s arm with warmth.*) Ask him, Katie. Come on, honey.
EDDIE	It's all right, I'm – (*He starts to go and she holds him.*)
BEATRICE	No, she wants to ask you. Come on, Katie, ask him. We'll have a party! What're we gonna do, hate each other? Come on!
CATHERINE	I'm gonna get married, Eddie. So if you wanna come, the wedding be on Saturday.
	Pause.
EDDIE	Okay. I only wanted the best for you, Katie. I hope you know that.
CATHERINE	Okay. (*She starts out again.*)
EDDIE	Catherine? (*She turns to him.*) I was tellin' Beatrice ... if you wanna go out, like ... I mean I realize maybe I kept you home too much. Because he's the first guy you ever knew, y'know? I mean now that you got a job, you might meet some fellas, and you get a different idea, y'know? I mean you could always come back to him, you're still only kids, the both of yiz. What's the hurry? Maybe you'll get around a little bit, you grow up a little more, maybe you'll see different in a couple of months. I mean you be surprised, it don't have to be him.
CATHERINE	No, we made it up already.
EDDIE	(*with increasing anxiety*) Katie, wait a minute.
CATHERINE	No, I made up my mind.
EDDIE	But you never knew no other fella, Katie! How could you make up your mind?
CATHERINE	'Cause I did. I don't want nobody else.
EDDIE	But, Katie, suppose he gets picked up.
CATHERINE	That's why we gonna do it right away. Soon as we

	finish the wedding he's goin' right over and start to be a citizen. I made up my mind, Eddie. I'm sorry. (*To* BEATRICE) Could I take two more pillow cases for the other guys?
BEATRICE	Sure, go ahead. Only don't let her forget where they came from.
	CATHERINE *goes into a bedroom.*
EDDIE	She's got other boarders up there?
BEATRICE	Yeah, there's two guys that just came over.
EDDIE	What do you mean, came over?
BEATRICE	From Italy. Lipari the butcher – his nephew. They come from Bari, they just got here yesterday. I didn't even know till Marco and Rodolfo moved up there before. (CATHERINE *enters, going toward exit with two pillow cases.*) It'll be nice, they could all talk together.
EDDIE	Catherine! (*She halts near the exit door. He takes in* BEATRICE *too.*) What're you, got no brains? You put them up there with two other submarines?
CATHERINE	Why?
EDDIE	(*in a driving fright and anger*) Why! How do you know they're not trackin' these guys? They'll come up for them and find Marco and Rodolfo! Get them out of the house!
BEATRICE	But they been here so long already –
EDDIE	How do you know what enemies Lipari's got? Which they'd love to stab him in the back?
CATHERINE	Well what'll I do with them?
EDDIE	The neighbourhood is full of rooms. Can't you stand to live a couple of blocks away from him? Get them out of the house!
CATHERINE	Well maybe tomorrow night I'll –
EDDIE	Not tomorrow, do it now. Catherine, you never mix yourself with somebody else's family! These guys get picked up, Lipari's liable to blame you or me and we got his whole family on our head. They got a temper, that family.
	Two men in overcoats appear outside, start into the house.
CATHERINE	How'm I gonna find a place tonight?
EDDIE	Will you stop arguin' with me and get them out! You think I'm always tryin' to fool you or sump'm? What's the matter with you, don't you believe I could think of your good? Did I ever ask sump'm for myself? You think I got no feelin's? I never told you nothin' in my life that wasn't for your good. Nothin'!

And look at the way you talk to me! Like I was an enemy!
Like I – (*A knock on the door. His head swerves. They all
stand motionless. Another knock.* EDDIE, *in a whisper,
pointing upstage.*) Go up the fire escape, get them out over
the back fence.

CATHERINE *stands motionless, uncomprehending.*

FIRST OFFICER   (*in the hall*) Immigration! Open up in there!

EDDIE   Go, go. Hurry up! (*She stands a moment staring at him in a
realized horror.*) Well, what're you lookin' at!

FIRST OFFICER   Open up!

EDDIE   (*calling toward door*) Who's that there?

FIRST OFFICER   Immigration, open up.

EDDIE *turns, looks at* BEATRICE. *She sits. Then he looks at*
CATHERINE. *With a sob of fury* CATHERINE *streaks into a
bedroom.*

Knock is repeated.

EDDIE   All right, take it easy, take it easy. (*He goes and opens the
door. The Officer steps inside.*) What's all this?

FIRST OFFICER   Where are they?

SECOND OFFICER *sweeps past and, glancing about, goes into
the kitchen.*

EDDIE   Where's who?

FIRST OFFICER   Come on, come on, where are they? (*He hurries into the
bedrooms.*)

EDDIE   Who? We got nobody here. (*He looks at* BEATRICE, *who turns
her head away. Pugnaciously, furious, he steps toward*
BEATRICE.) What's the matter with *you?*

FIRST OFFICER *enters from the bedroom, calls to the kitchen.*

FIRST OFFICER   Dominick?

Enter SECOND OFFICER *from kitchen.*

SECOND OFFICER   Maybe it's a different apartment.

FIRST OFFICER   There's only two more floors up there. I'll take the front,
you go up the fire escape. I'll let you in. Watch your step
up there.

SECOND OFFICER   Okay, right, Charley. (FIRST OFFICER *goes out apartment
door and runs up the stairs.*) This is Four-forty-one, isn't it?

EDDIE   That's right.

SECOND OFFICER *goes out into the kitchen.*

EDDIE *turns to* BEATRICE. *She looks at him now and sees his
terror.*

BEATRICE   (*weakened with fear*) Oh, Jesus, Eddie.

EDDIE   What's the matter with *you*?

BEATRICE   (*pressing her palms against her face*) Oh, my God, my God.

EDDIE   What're you, accusin' me?

BEATRICE   (*her final thrust is to turn toward him instead of running from him*) My God, what did you do?

             Many steps on the outer stair draw his attention. We see the FIRST OFFICER *descending, with* MARCO, *behind him* RODOLFO, *and* CATHERINE *and the two strange immigrants, followed by* SECOND OFFICER. BEATRICE *hurries to door.*

CATHERINE   (*backing down stairs, fighting with* FIRST OFFICER; *as they appear on the stairs*) What do yiz want from them? They work, that's all. They're boarders upstairs, they work on the piers.

BEATRICE   (*to* FIRST OFFICER) Ah, Mister, what do you want from them, who do they hurt?

CATHERINE   (*pointing to* RODOLFO) They ain't no submarines, he was born in Philadelphia.

FIRST OFFICER   Step aside, lady.

CATHERINE   What do you mean? You can't just come in a house and –

FIRST OFFICER   All right, take it easy. (*To* RODOLFO) What street were you born in Philadelphia?

CATHERINE   What do you mean, what street? Could you tell me what street you were born?

FIRST OFFICER   Sure. Four blocks away, One-eleven Union Street. Let's go fellas.

CATHERINE   (*fending him off* RODOLFO) No, you can't! Now, get outa here!

FIRST OFFICER   Look, girlie, if they're all right they'll be out tomorrow. If they're illegal they go back where they came from. If you want, get yourself a lawyer, although I'm tellin' you now you're wasting your money. Let's get them in the car, Dom. (*To the men*) Andiamo, andiamo, let's go.

             The men start, but MARCO *hangs back.*

BEATRICE   (*from doorway*) Who're they hurtin', for God's sake, what do you want from them? They're starvin' over there, what do you want! Marco!

             MARCO *suddenly breaks from the group and dashes into the*

                   room and faces EDDIE; BEATRICE *and* FIRST OFFICER *rush in as*
                   MARCO *spits into* EDDIE'*s face.*

                   CATHERINE *runs into hallway and throws herself into*
                   RODOLFO'*s arms.* EDDIE, *with an enraged cry, lunges for*
                   MARCO.

EDDIE   Oh, you mother's –!

                   FIRST OFFICER *quickly intercedes and pushes* EDDIE *from*
                   MARCO, *who stands there accusingly.*

FIRST OFFICER (*between them, pushing* EDDIE *from* MARCO) Cut it out!

EDDIE   (*over the* FIRST OFFICER'*s shoulder, to* MARCO) I'll kill you for
                   that, you son of a bitch!

FIRST OFFICER Hey! (*Shakes him.*) Stay in here now, don't come out,
                   don't bother him. You hear me! Don't come out, fella.
                   For an instant there is silence. Then FIRST OFFICER *turns and*
                   takes MARCO'*s arm and then gives a last, informative look at*
                   EDDIE. *As he and* MARCO *are going out into the hall,* EDDIE
                   erupts.

EDDIE   I don't forget that, Marco! You hear what I'm sayin'?
                   Out in the hall, FIRST OFFICER *and* MARCO *go down the stairs.*
                   Now, in the street, LOUIS, MIKE, *and several neighbours*
                   including the butcher, LIPARI – *a stout, intense, middle-aged*
                   man – are gathering around the stoop.
                   LIPARI, *the butcher, walks over to the two strange men and*
                   kisses them. His wife, keening, goes and kisses their hands.
                   EDDIE *is emerging from the house shouting after* MARCO.
                   BEATRICE *is trying to restrain him.*

EDDIE   That's the thanks I get? Which I took the blankets off my
                   bed for yiz? You gonna apologize to me, Marco! *Marco!*

FIRST OFFICER (*in the doorway with* MARCO) All right, lady, let them go.
                   Get in the car, fellas, it's right over there.

                   RODOLFO *is almost carrying the sobbing* CATHERINE *off up the*
                   street, left.

CATHERINE   He was born in Philadelphia! What do you want from him?

FIRST OFFICER Step aside, lady, come on now …

                   The SECOND OFFICER *has moved off with the two strange men.*
                   MARCO, *taking advantage of the* FIRST OFFICER'*s being*
                   occupied with CATHERINE, *suddenly frees himself and points*
                   back at EDDIE.

MARCO   That one! I accuse that one!

                   EDDIE *brushes* BEATRICE *aside and rushes out to the stoop.*

58 A VIEW FROM THE BRIDGE

FIRST OFFICER (*grabbing him and moving him quickly off up the left street*) Come on!

MARCO (*as he is taken off, pointing back at* EDDIE) That one! He killed my children! That one stole the food from my children!

MARCO *is gone. The crowd has turned to* EDDIE.

EDDIE (*to* LIPARI *and wife*) He's crazy! I give them the blankets off my bed. Six months I kept them like my own brothers!

LIPARI, *the butcher, turns and starts up left with his arm around his wife.*

EDDIE Lipari! (*He follows* LIPARI *up left.*) For Christ's sake, I kept them, I give them the blankets off my bed!

LIPARI *and wife exit.* EDDIE *turns and starts crossing down right to* LOUIS *and* MIKE.

EDDIE Louis! *Louis!*

LOUIS *barely turns, then walks off and exits down right with* MIKE. *Only* BEATRICE *is left on the stoop.* CATHERINE *now returns, blank-eyed, from offstage and the car.* EDDIE *calls after* LOUIS *and* MIKE.

EDDIE He's gonna take that back. He's gonna take that back or I'll kill him! You hear me? I'll kill him! (*He exits up street calling.*)

There is a pause of darkness before the lights rise, on the reception room of a prison. MARCO *is seated;* ALFIERI, CATHERINE, *and* RODOLFO *standing.*

ALFIERI I'm waiting, Marco, what do you say?

RODOLFO Marco never hurt anybody.

ALFIERI I can bail you out until your hearing comes up. But I'm not going to do it, you understand me? Unless I have your promise. You're an honourable man, I will believe your promise. Now what do you say?

MARCO In my country he would be dead now. He would not live this long.

ALFIERI All right, Rodolfo – you come with me now.

RODOLFO No! Please, Mister. Marco – promise the man. Please, I want you to watch the wedding. How can I be married and you're in here? Please, you're not going to do anything; you know you're not.

MARCO *is silent.*

CATHERINE (*kneeling left of* MARCO) Marco, don't you understand?

He can't bail you out if you're gonna do something bad. To hell with Eddie. Nobody is gonna talk to him again if he lives to a hundred. Everybody knows you spit in his face, that's enough, isn't it? Give me the satisfaction – I want you at the wedding. You got a wife and kids, Marco. You could be workin' till the hearing comes up, instead of layin' around here.

MARCO   (*to* ALFIERI) I have no chance?

ALFIERI   (*crosses to behind* MARCO) No, Marco. You're going back. The hearing is a formality, that's all.

MARCO   But him? There is a chance, eh?

ALFIERI   When she marries him he can start to become an American. They permit that, if the wife is born here.

MARCO   (*looking at* RODOLFO) Well – we did something. (*He lays a palm on* RODOLFO'*s arm and* RODOLFO *covers it.*)

RODOLFO   Marco, tell the man.

MARCO   (*pulling his hand away*) What will I tell him? He knows such a promise is dishonourable.

ALFIERI   To promise not to kill is not dishonourable.

MARCO   (*looking at* ALFIERI) No?

ALFIERI   No.

MARCO   (*gesturing with his head – this is a new idea*) Then what is done with such a man?

ALFIERI   Nothing. If he obeys the law, he lives. That's all.

MARCO   (*rises, turns to* ALFIERI) The law? All the law is not in a book.

ALFIERI   Yes. In a book. There is no other law.

MARCO   (*his anger rising*) He degraded my brother. My blood. He robbed my children, he mocks my work. I work to come here, mister!

ALFIERI   I know, Marco –

MARCO   There is no law for that? Where is the law for that?

ALFIERI   There is none.

MARCO   (*shaking his head, sitting*) I don't understand this country.

ALFIERI   Well? What is your answer? You have five or six weeks you could work. Or else you sit here. What do you say to me?

MARCO   (*lowers his eyes. It almost seems he is ashamed*) All right.

ALFIERI   You won't touch him. This is your promise.
Slight pause.

MARCO   Maybe he wants to apologize to me.

MARCO *is staring away.* ALFIERI *takes one of his hands.*

ALFIERI   This is not God, Marco. You hear? Only God makes justice.

MARCO   All right.

ALFIERI   (*nodding, not with assurance*) Good! Catherine, Rodolfo, Marco, let us go.

CATHERINE *kisses* RODOLFO *and* MARCO, *then kisses* ALFIERI *'s hand.*

CATHERINE   I'll get Beatrice and meet you at the church. (*She leaves quickly.*)

ALFIERI   Only God, Marco.

MARCO *turns and walks out.* ALFIERI *with a certain processional tread leaves the stage. The lights dim out.*

The lights rise in the apartment. EDDIE *is alone in the rocker, rocking back and forth in little surges. Pause. Now* BEATRICE *emerges from a bedroom. She is in her best clothes, wearing a hat.*

BEATRICE   (*with fear, going to* EDDIE) I'll be back in about an hour, Eddie. All right?

EDDIE   (*quietly, almost inaudibly, as though drained*) What, have I been talkin' to myself?

BEATRICE   Eddie, for God's sake, it's her wedding.

EDDIE   Didn't you hear what I told you? You walk out that door to that wedding you ain't comin' back here, Beatrice.

BEATRICE   Why! What do you want?

EDDIE   I want my respect. Didn't you ever hear of that? From my wife?

CATHERINE *enters from bedroom.*

CATHERINE   It's after three; we're supposed to be there already, Beatrice. The priest won't wait.

BEATRICE   Eddie. It's her wedding. There'll be nobody there from her family. For my sister let me go. I'm goin' for my sister.

EDDIE   (*as though hurt*) Look, I been arguin' with you all day already, Beatrice, and I said what I'm gonna say. He's gonna come here and apologize to me or nobody from this house is goin' into that church today. Now if that's more to you than I

am, then go. But don't come back. You be on my side
or on their side, that's all.

CATHERINE (*suddenly*) Who the hell do you think you are?

BEATRICE Sssh!

CATHERINE You got no more right to tell nobody nothin'! Nobody!
The rest of your life, nobody!

BEATRICE Shut up, Katie! (*She turns* CATHERINE *around.*)

CATHERINE You're gonna come with me!

BEATRICE I can't Katie, I can't …

CATHERINE How can you listen to him? This rat!

BEATRICE (*shaking* CATHERINE) Don't you call him that!

CATHERINE (*clearing from* BEATRICE) What're you scared of? He's a
rat! He belongs in the sewer!

BEATRICE Stop it!

CATHERINE (*weeping*) He bites people when they sleep! He comes
when nobody's lookin' and poisons decent people. In
the garbage he belongs!

EDDIE *seems about to pick up the table and fling it at her.*

BEATRICE No, Eddie! Eddie! (*To* CATHERINE) Then we all belong in
the garbage. You, and me too. Don't say that. Whatever
happened we all done it, and don't you ever forget it,
Catherine. (*She goes to* CATHERINE.) Now go, go to your
wedding, Katie, I'll stay home. Go. God bless you, God
bless your children.

Enter RODOLFO.

RODOLFO Eddie?

EDDIE Who said you could come in here? Get outa here!

RODOLFO Marco is coming, Eddie. (*Pause.* BEATRICE *raises her
hands in terror.* RODOLFO *advances into the room.*)
Catherine, I think it is better we go. Come with me.

CATHERINE Eddie, go away please.

BEATRICE (*quietly*) Eddie. Let's go someplace. Come. You and me.
(*He has not moved.*) I don't want you to be here when
he comes. I'll get your coat.

EDDIE Where? Where am I goin'? This is my house.

BEATRICE (*crying out*) What's the use of it! He's crazy now, you
know the way they get, what good is it! You got nothin'
against Marco, you always liked Marco!

EDDIE	I got nothin' against Marco? Which he called me a rat in front of the whole neighbourhood? Which he said I killed his children! Where you been?
RODOLFO	(*quiet suddenly, stepping up to* EDDIE) It is my fault, Eddie. Everything. I wish to apologize. It was wrong that I do not ask your permission. I kiss your hand. (*He reaches for* EDDIE*'s hand, but* EDDIE *snaps it away from him.*)
BEATRICE	Eddie, he's apologizing!
RODOLFO	I have made all our troubles. But you have insult me too. Maybe God understand why you did that to me. Maybe you did not mean to insult me at all –
BEATRICE	Listen to him! Eddie, listen what he's tellin' you!
RODOLFO	I think, maybe when Marco comes, if we can tell him we are comrades now, and we have no more argument between us. Then maybe Marco will not –
EDDIE	Now, listen –
CATHERINE	Eddie, give him a chance!
BEATRICE	What do you want! Eddie, what do you want!
EDDIE	I want my name! He didn't take my name; he's only a punk. Marco's got my name – (*to* RODOLFO) and you can run tell him, kid, that he's gonna give it back to me in front of this neighbourhood, or we have it out. (*Hoisting up his pants*) Come on, where is he? Take me to him.
BEATRICE	Eddie, listen –
EDDIE	I heard enough! Come on, let's go!
BEATRICE	Only blood is good? He kissed your hand!
EDDIE	What he does don't mean nothin' to nobody! (*To* RODOLFO) Come on!
BEATRICE	(*barring his way to the stairs*) What's gonna mean somethin'? Eddie, listen to me. Who could give you your name? Listen to me, I love you, I'm talkin' to you, I love you; if Marco'll kiss your hand outside, if he goes on his knees, what is he got to give you? That's not what you want.
EDDIE	Don't bother me!
BEATRICE	You want somethin' else, Eddie, and you can never have her!
CATHERINE	(*in horror*) B.!
EDDIE	(*shocked, horrified, his fists clenching*) Beatrice!

MARCO *appears outside, walking toward the door from a distant point.*

BEATRICE   (*crying out, weeping*) The truth is not as bad as blood, Eddie! I'm tellin' you the truth – tell her good-bye forever!

EDDIE   (*crying out in agony*) That's what you think of me – that I would have such a thoughts? (*His fists clench his head as though it will burst.*)

MARCO   (*calling near the door outside*) Eddie Carbone!

EDDIE *swerves about; all stand transfixed for an instant. People appear outside.*

EDDIE   (*as though flinging his challenge*) Yeah, Marco! Eddie Carbone. Eddie Carbone. Eddie Carbone. (*He goes up the stairs and emerges from the apartment.* RODOLFO *streaks up and out past him and runs to* MARCO.)

RODOLFO   No, Marco, please! Eddie, please, he has children! You will kill a family!

BEATRICE   Go in the house! Eddie, go in the house!

EDDIE   (*he gradually comes to address the people*) Maybe he come to apologize to me. Heh, Marco? For what you said about me in front of the neighbourhood? (*He is incensing himself and little bits of laughter even escape him as his eyes are murderous and he cracks his knuckles in his hands with a strange sort of relaxation.*) He knows that ain't right. To do like that? To a man? Which I put my roof over their head and my food in their mouth? Like in the Bible? Strangers I never seen in my whole life? To come out of the water and grab a girl for a passport? To go and take from your own family like from the stable – and never a word to me? And now accusations in the bargain! (*Directly to* MARCO) Wipin' the neighbourhood with my name like a dirty rag! I want my name, Marco. (*He is moving now, carefully, toward* MARCO.) Now gimme my name and we go together to the wedding.

BEATRICE *and* CATHERINE   (*keening*) Eddie! Eddie, don't! Eddie!

EDDIE   No, Marco knows what's right from wrong. Tell the people, Marco, tell them what a liar you are! (*He has his arms spread and* MARCO *is spreading his.*) Come on, liar, you know what you done! (*He lunges for* MARCO *as a great hushed shout goes up from the people.*)

MARCO *strikes* EDDIE *beside the neck.*

MARCO   Animal! You go on your knees to me!

EDDIE *goes* down *with the blow and* MARCO *starts to raise a foot to stomp him when* EDDIE *springs a knife into his hand and* MARCO *steps back.* LOUIS *rushes in toward* EDDIE.

LOUIS   Eddie, for Christ's sake!

EDDIE *raises the knife and* LOUIS *halts and steps back.*

EDDIE   You lied about me, Marco. Now say it. Come on now, say it!

MARCO   Anima-a-a-l!

EDDIE *lunges with the knife.* MARCO *grabs his arm, turning the blade inward and pressing it home as the women and* LOUIS *and* MIKE *rush in and separate them, and* EDDIE, *the knife still in his hand, falls to his knees before* MARCO. *The two women support him for a moment, calling his name again and again.*

CATHERINE Eddie, I never meant to do nothing bad to you.

EDDIE   Then why – Oh, B.!

BEATRICE   Yes, yes!

EDDIE   My B.!

He dies in her arms, and BEATRICE *covers him with her body.* ALFIERI, *who is in the crowd, turns out to the audience. The lights have gone down, leaving him in a glow, while behind him the dull prayers of the people and the keening of the women continue.*

ALFIERI   Most of the time now we settle for half and I like it better. But the truth is holy, and even as I know how wrong he was, and his death useless, I tremble, for I confess that something perversely pure calls to me from his memory – not purely good, but himself purely, for he allowed himself to be wholly known and for that I think I will love him more than all my sensible clients. And yet, it is better to settle for half, it must be! And so I mourn him – I admit it – with a certain … alarm.

CURTAIN

QUESTIONS AND EXPLORATIONS

1 Keeping Track

The questions in this section are intended to help your reading and understanding of the play in the areas of plot, character, interaction and structure. They may be used as you read the play or afterwards, for discussion or for writing. Some are developed and expanded in the *Explorations* section.

Act One

1 What are the themes raised by Alfieri in his prologue?
2 What is Eddie's attitude to the changes in Catherine? Why?
3 How would Catherine react to Eddie's concern?
4 What is important about the arrival of Beatrice's cousins?
5 What do we learn of the relationship between Eddie and Beatrice?
6 How does Eddie react to the news of Catherine's job? Why?
7 Why does Eddie change his mind about her job? And how does Catherine's reaction make him feel?
8 How does the atmosphere at the meal table change when they start to talk about Beatrice's cousins?
9 Why is the story of Vinny Bolzano important?
10 Why does Beatrice tell Eddie he is 'mad'?
11 What is Eddie thinking as he sits and smokes alone?
12 How would Tony, Marco and Rodolfo arrive?
13 How does the family greet the brothers?
14 What differences are noticeable between Marco and Rodolfo?

15   How does Eddie show his opinion of Rodolfo?

16   What are Marco's and Rodolfo's ambitions?

17   How do Catherine and Rodolfo show their developing attitudes to each other?

18   How does Eddie react to Rodolfo's singing?

19   Why does Eddie send Catherine to change her shoes? How does she react?

20   What is Eddie thinking as Catherine serves Rodolfo sugar?

21   What is the trouble 'that will not go away'?

22   What is Eddie's opinion of Rodolfo?

23   What are the problems between Eddie and Beatrice?

24   What reputations do Marco and Rodolfo gain?

25   How does Eddie react to Catherine and Rodolfo's return?

26   What is Eddie afraid of for Catherine?

27   Why does Eddie leave the house?

28   How does Catherine react to what Beatrice tells her?

29   What are Eddie's feelings as he speaks to Alfieri?

30   What does Alfieri try to make Eddie understand?

31   How does Alfieri feel after the interview?

32   How do Rodolfo and Marco react to Eddie's criticism?

33   Why does Catherine invite Rodolfo to dance?

34   How do Beatrice, Marco and Eddie each react to this?

35   What is Eddie trying to do as he boxes with Rodolfo?

36   What is Marco trying to prove by lifting the chair? How would both Eddie and the others react?

Act Two

1   How would Alfieri speak his prologue to Act Two?

2   What makes Rodolfo furious?

3   And what upsets Catherine?

4   Why does Eddie kiss Catherine?

5   Why does Eddie kiss Rodolfo?

6   What does Eddie threaten he will do to Rodolfo?

7   How does Eddie behave in his interview with Alfieri?

8   What does Alfieri fear for Eddie?

9   How does Eddie feel that Beatrice is treating him?

10 How does Eddie react to the news that Catherine is to marry the next week?

11 How do Catherine and Eddie react to each other?

12 Why is Catherine determined to marry soon?

13 What is Eddie afraid of when he learns that two more illegal immigrants are in the house?

14 How do the members of the family react to the arrival of the Immigration Officers?

15 Why does Marco spit in Eddie's face?

16 How does Eddie react? Why?

17 How does the neighbourhood treat Eddie? Why?

18 Why does Marco want revenge so badly?

19 How does Beatrice feel as she prepares for the wedding?

20 Why does Rodolfo warn Eddie about Marco?

21 What does Eddie mean when he says 'Marco's got my name'?

22 Why does Beatrice tell Eddie the truth?

23 How does the neighbourhood react to the fight?

24 What does Alfieri mean by 'it is better to settle for half'?

2 Explorations

The questions in this section are more detailed and rely on your having read the whole play. Some of the questions develop ideas from the *Keeping Track* section. Because they tend to be more detailed, they offer the opportunity to develop ideas into written, oral or practical coursework assignments. Some will require a close knowledge of the play; others will require a more imaginative response.

A Characters

Eddie

1 'Believe me, Eddie, you got a lotta credit comin' to you.' How and why is Eddie respected in the neighbourhood?

2 'Look, you gotta get used to it, she's no baby no more.' Trace and explain the development of Eddie's feelings for Catherine.

3 'I want my respect.' What are the stages of the collapse of Eddie's marriage to Beatrice? How does this make Eddie feel?

4 'His eyes were like tunnels …' Explain the effects of the events of the play upon Eddie.

5 If Eddie had not died … Draft and present the statement Eddie would have made to the Immigration Bureau about the events of the play. Use language appropriate to the character to show your understanding.

Beatrice

1 'What are you mad at me lately?' How does Beatrice show her anxiety about Eddie?

2 'When am I going to be a wife again, Eddie?' How is Beatrice affected by the collapse of her marriage to Eddie?

3 Plan, draft and present the statement that Beatrice would make to the police about the events of the play. Use language appropriate to the character to show your understanding.

Catherine

1 'Now don't get mad, kid.' How does Catherine react to Eddie's treatment of her in the course of the play?

2 'I don't know how to talk to you.' How would Catherine show her development into adulthood?

3 'Why are you so afraid of him?' Explain Catherine's attitude to Eddie as it develops through the course of the play.

4 'Eddie, I never meant to do nothing bad to you.' How is Catherine affected, finally, by the events of the play?

5 Plan, draft and present the statement that Catherine would make to the police about the events of the play. Use language appropriate to the character to show your understanding.

Marco

1 'Marco goes around like a man; nobody kids Marco.' How does Marco behave and present himself in the course of the play?

2 'My brother is desperate, but not me.' Explain the differences between Marco and Rodolfo.

3 'I don't understand this country.' What is it about America that Marco does not understand? Why?

4 Plan, draft and present the statement that Marco would make to the police about the events of the play. Use language appropriate to the character to show your understanding.

Rodolfo

1 'When you have no wife you have dreams.' What are Rodolfo's priorities in coming to the United States?

2   'That's a nice kid? He gives me the heeby-jeebies.' Explain Eddie's reaction to Rodolfo.

3   'I show you what I can be!' How does Rodolfo change as a result of the events of the play?

4   Plan, draft and present the statement that Rodolfo would make to the police about the events of the play. Use language appropriate to the character to show your understanding.

Alfieri

1   'The law is only a word for what has a right to happen.' Why is Alfieri unable to influence the events of the play?

2   'Now we settle for half, and I like it better.' What is Alfieri's attitude to the events he witnesses in the play?

3   Plan, draft and present the statement that Alfieri would make to the police about the events of the play. Use language appropriate to the character to show your understanding.

General

1   The whole neighbourhood was cryin'…' Explain the neighbourhood's reaction to the events of the play.

2   Create the front page story that the Red Hook Reporter would publish reporting the events portrayed in the play. Include comments from the major characters as necessary.

B In Performance

1   Draw up a set design brief for the play. What set, furniture and props would be required in order to create the necessary atmosphere for the benefit of an audience?

2   Draw up a costume design brief for the play. How would you use costume to reveal character for the benefit of the audience?

3 Select one of the major characters from the play. Which aspects of that character would you need, as an actor/actress, to highlight in performance? How would you use voice, gesture and movement to achieve this?

Present your ideas in the form of notes to an actor playing that part.

4 Select the character of either Eddie, Beatrice or Catherine. Explain how an actor/actress playing your chosen character could show the changes that occur in that character during the course of the play.

5 Select a brief scene of dramatic tension from the play. Prepare notes to show how, as a director, you would want this moment to be played by your actors. Concentrate on both the actions and interactions of the characters to show the development of the scene.

6 What reaction does Miller intend the audience to have to the content of the play? How does he prepare the audience for what is to follow ... and is he successful in achieving his intentions?

7 Create and present a poster to advertise a production of the play for your local theatre. How would you interest and attract a potential audience, without telling them too much about the play itself?

C Themes and Criticism

1 'What are you worried about? She could take care of herself.' What lessons are drawn in the play about parents or guardians?

2 'The law is only a word for what has a right to happen.' What is the role of the law in the world of the play?

3 'Most of the time now we settle for half and I like it better.' Giving examples, explain how justice is important in the world of the play. What moral does Miller intend us to draw?

4   'I want my name!' How far does pride dictate the events of the play?

5   'You won't have a friend in the world, Eddie!' What is the importance of loyalty in the world of the play?

6   'I'm tellin' you the truth – tell her goodbye forever!' By referring to the text, show how Eddie Carbone brings his fate upon himself.

7   'Eddie, I never meant to do nothing bad to you.' How much is Catherine to blame for the events which lead to the death of Eddie Carbone?

8   'Justice is very important here.' Show how the characters' need for justice leads to the climax of the play.

Glossary

Bibliography

Other works

Other plays of Arthur Miller's related in theme to *A View from the Bridge* are: *All My Sons, Death of a Salesman* and *The Crucible.*

Miller's autobiography, *Timebends*, was published in 1987 by Methuen.

Criticism

Critical studies which may be of use include:

Arthur Miller	Ronald Hayman	Unger 1972
Miller: A Study of His Plays	Dennis Welland	Methuen 1979
Miller the Playwright	Dennis Welland	Methuen 1993
File on Miller	ed. Simon Trussler	Methuen 1986

IRISH NAMES

CHOOSING A NAME FOR YOUR BABY

Compiled by Felicity Trotman

Gill Books

IRISH NAMES is the indispensable guide for prospective parents trying to select a name for their child. In recent years, the trend for many people has been to choose names with strong historical connections and the rich seam of religious, mythological and legendary Irish links provides an unusual and vivid wealth of material.

The Celts' early influence in Ireland was considerable and remained strong for nearly 1,000 years. Their legacy is still with us in the many artefacts to be seen in Ireland today with strong Celtic associations and in Celtic names, which remain very popular both in Ireland and abroad. The spread of Christianity to Ireland brought about the creation of many saints, whose names, with their colourful associations, still appeal to modern parents. Viking raids on Ireland began in the late 8th century and this turbulent period produced its own fund of strong and evocative names which recall the adventures and drama of the times.

The Anglo-Norman period that followed left behind yet more unusual and intriguing names which reflect the characteristics of these two races, thus mixing the medley even more. Protestant settlers from Scotland also brought with them Scottish names which were absorbed into the Irish culture.

Elegantly designed and decorated, this comprehensive selection covers not only the history of traditional names but also mentions contemporary personalities who have Irish names. The range provided here will intrigue and delight all readers!

Agnes

Natasha

Yvonne

Frances

Alexandra Jean

Aisling Amy

Eve

Joan Charlotte

Dorothy Aoibheann

Cara Angela

Nessa Valerie

Deirdre

 ## Abigail, Abbie
Aibigéal

Abigail is Hebrew and means 'father rejoiced'. In the Bible, Abigail was the beautiful wife of Nabal the Calebite, who married King David after the death of Nabal. By the 18th century, Abigail had become the name for a maidservant. It was particularly common in West Cork.

 ## Adele

Adele is a French version of an old German word, meaning 'noble'. St Adela was a Merovingian princess, the daughter of Dagobert II (656–705), king of the Franks, and sister of St Irmina. After her husband Alberie died, she founded and became abbess of a convent at Pfalzel near Trier (now in western Germany).

 ## Agnes

Agnes comes from a Greek word that means 'pure' or 'holy', but has also been associated with the Latin *agnus*, meaning 'lamb'. Agnes Mary Clerke (1842–1907), born in Skibbereen, wrote the authoritative *A History of Astronomy During the Nineteenth Century* in 1885. The lunar crater Clerke is named after her.

Aideen
Etaoin

Some scholars believe Etain, or Etaoin, may be derived from a word meaning 'jealousy'. Aideen is the modern version of the name. Aideen was married to Oscar, a grandson of Fionn Mac Cumhaill, and she died of a broken heart when he was killed in battle. There have been many women called Etaoin in ancient Irish legend and history. The best known was the very beautiful Etain Echraide, loved by Midir, a king of the magical Tuatha de Danaan. Midir's wife turned Etain into a fly, but after many adventures she was reunited with Midir.

Aifric

The name itself is credited with the meaning 'pleasant'. Aifric, or Affreca, was the daughter of Gottred, king of Man. In 1180 she married John de Courcy, a Norman soldier who conquered and ruled part of Ulster. Affreca founded Grey Abbey on Strangford Lough, Co. Down. Two abbesses of Kildare were called Aifric.

Ailbhe

Ailbhe means 'white'. It is a name that can be used by men and women. The two saints Ailbhe were men. Ailbe Grúadbrece was one of the wives of Fionn Mac Cumhaill and daughter of Cormac Mac Airt.

Aisling, Aislinn
Ashling

Aisling means 'dream' or 'vision'. It has only been used as a name very recently, as part of the Irish Revival of the late 19th and early 20th centuries. Aisling is a kind of Irish poetry, much composed from the 17th to the 19th centuries. In these poems, the poet meets a woman (a symbol of Ireland) when out walking. She laments the current state of the Irish people and predicts an upturn in fortune for them. Often, the poet is left with dreams of the woman forever after.

Alanna, Alannah
There are two possible meanings of this name. It could be a female form of Alan, a Gaelic name meaning 'spirit' or 'elf'. Alanna could also come from the Irish endearment 'a leanbh', meaning 'child' or 'darling child'.

Alexandra
Alexandra is the female version of Alexander, which comes from the Greek and means 'defender of men'. St Alexandra was the wife of the Emperor Diocletian. She was so impressed by St George's courage when he was martyred that she became a Christian (some say she was already secretly a Christian). Condemned under the terms of her husband's persecution, she was to be beheaded. She asked to sit down and died quietly before the sentence could be carried out.

Alice
Ailis, Ailís
Alice is related to Adelaide, which comes from old German and means 'of noble birth' or 'princess'. It was probably introduced to Ireland by the Normans.

Alison
Allsún
Alison is a pet form of Alice [see Alice]. Some assign it a mixed meaning taken from Alice and Louise, leading to 'truthful warrior maid'.

Alma
The Irish name Almha means 'all good'. The modern name Alma can be tracked back in different ways. The Battle of Alma was fought in 1854 during the Crimean War; Alma, as used in Spenser's *The Faerie Queene* (1590–6), comes from the Italian word for 'soul'; or the name may have come from the Latin meaning 'kind' or 'nurturing'. Almha was one of the magical Tuatha Dé Danaan. She was also the daughter of a warrior.

Amy, Aimee
Amy comes from a French word and means 'beloved'.

Andrea

Andrea is the female form of Andrew, a Greek name meaning 'strong' or 'courageous'. When ascribed to a female it is given the meaning 'the epitome of feminine charm and beauty'.

Angela
Aingeal

Angela is Greek and means 'messenger'. St Angela of Foligno (1248–1309) was a mystic whose spiritual writings have been influential. Italian St Angela Merici (1474–1540) founded the Company of St Ursula, or Ursulines, an order of teaching nuns who worked with children in their homes.

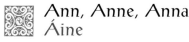

Ann, Anne, Anna
Áine

Ann is Hebrew and means 'grace' or 'he has favoured me'. In the Bible, Hannah – a version of Anne – was the mother of the prophet Samuel. Ann was also the name of the Virgin Mary's mother, who is regarded as a saint.

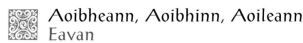

Aoibheann, Aoibhinn, Aoileann
Eavan

Aoibheann means 'radiance', 'spark', or 'fire'. In ancient Irish legend, Aibell (an old spelling) was a goddess, or fairy queen, who lived in a mound at Craig Liath near Killaloe, Co. Clare. A jealous rival turned her into a white cat. The mother of St Enda of Aran was called Aoibhin. Eavan Boland, a poet, is the most well-known bearer of the name today.

Aoife
Eva

Aoife means 'beautiful', or 'radiant'. Many women in ancient Irish myths and legends have been called Aoife. In the story of the Children of Lir, Aoife was the wicked stepmother who turned her stepchildren into swans. Another Aoife loved a man called Ilbrec, but a jealous rival transformed her into a crane. As a bird, she spent hundreds of years in the kingdom of the sea-god Manánan Mac Lir.

Barbara
Báirbre

Barbara is Greek and means 'foreign woman'. St Barbara was so beautiful that her father locked her in a tower, to discourage suitors. When she became a Christian, he killed her but was instantly struck by lightning and burnt to ashes. St Barbara is the patron saint of architects, gunners, masons and miners. It is a popular Gaelic name in Connacht.

Bernadette

Bernadette is the female form of Bernard, which is old German and means 'strong bear' or 'strong as a bear'. St Bernadette (1844–79) had 18 visions of the Virgin Mary at Lourdes, who told her to ask for prayers and penitence. A spring of water at Lourdes is believed to have healing properties and it has become a centre of pilgrimage for those seeking relief from pain and illness.

Bláthnaid, Bláthnait

Bláthnait means 'little flower'. In ancient Irish legend, Bláthnait fell in love with Cúchulainn, and helped him to ambush and kill her husband Cú Roí Mac Daire, king of Munster. But Cú Roí's poet took vengeance on Bláthnait. When he saw her standing near a cliff he rushed at her, grasped her in his arms, then leaped over the cliff so they were both killed.

Brenda

Some people believe Brenda is the female form of Brendan. However, scholars believe it is Norse, and means 'brand' or 'sword'.

Brianna

Brianna is the female form of Brian. Some scholars believe Brianna is a Breton word meaning 'dignity' or 'pride', while others think it is a Celtic word meaning 'high' or 'noble'. It is a name that has been devised quite recently.

Bridget, Brigid, Breeda Bríghid, Bríd

Bridget means 'the high one' or 'exalted'. Brigit was originally an Irish goddess who looked after fire (especially blacksmiths') and poetry. There are several saints called Bridget. St Brigid of Kildare (around 450–523) is the most important saint in Ireland after St Patrick. She founded a community of nuns – the first for women in Ireland – at Kildare, and was its abbess, renowned for her generosity. Many stories were later told about her, some of them Christianised versions of stories told about the goddess Brigit. After Brigid died, her remains were taken to Downpatrick, where they were said to be buried with St Patrick. Her feast day is 1 February, the first day of spring in the Celtic calendar.

Bronagh Brónach

Bronagh means 'sorrowful'. It is sometimes used as a Celtic equivalent of the name Dolores. St Bronagh (7th century) gave her name to Kilbroney, Co. Down. Little is known about her life, but her bell is in the Catholic church in Rostrevor, Co. Down, and her crozier is in the National Museum, Dublin. Her name has remained popular in Co. Down for centuries.

Caoimhe
Keeva

Caoimhe is the female version of Caomhín (Kevin). Caoimhe means 'gentleness', 'loveliness' or 'grace'. St Caoimhe was a virgin, celebrated at Killeavy, Co. Down, though nothing else is known about her. The name has seen a rise in popularity in recent years.

Cara

From the Irish word for 'friend', possibly of Irish-American origin. In Italian Cara means 'beloved'.

Carmel

Carmel is Hebrew and means 'garden'. Carmel is the name of a mountain in the Holy Land. Traditionally, it was often visited by the Virgin Mary and her baby son, and as a female name Carmel refers to Our Lady of Mount Carmel. Later, many hermits lived on the mountain. They were eventually organised into the Carmelite order of monks.

Carol, Caroline

Carol and Caroline are female versions of Carolus, the Latin form of Charles, a German name meaning 'strong' or 'manly'. In its feminine form it is given the attributes 'little woman, born to command' – being the power behind the throne.

Catherine, Katherine
Caitrín, Caitríona, Tríona, Ríona

Catherine (or Katherine) is Greek, and means 'pure'. Catherine McAuley (1787–1841) was the Irish founder of the House of Mercy, which educated the poor, and of the Sisters of Mercy. Kitty O'Shea (1846–1921) caused the downfall of Charles Stewart Parnell when he was cited as co-respondent by her husband in divorce proceedings. The short version, Kate, has been popular in Ireland for many years.

Cathleen, Kathleen
Caitlín

Cathleen is an Anglicised version of Caitlín, which is the Irish form of Katherine [see Katherine]. Cathleen Ní Houlihan is a personification of Ireland, used by the poet WB Yeats.

Charlotte
Seárlait

Charlotte is a French female form of Charles, a German name meaning 'strong' or 'manly'. Charlotte Brontë (1816–55), of Irish extraction, wrote several novels, including *Jane Eyre*. Charlotte Despard (1844–1939) was a novelist, suffragist and social reformer. She established health centres for the poor in London, then extended her work for the poor in Dublin. She was a member of Sinn Féin during the Civil War.

Chloe

Chloe is Greek and means 'a young green shoot'. It was one of the names of Demeter, the Greek goddess of fertility and harvest. In poetry, the name is often given to country girls. Modern-day examples include the fashion house Chloé, notable for its designs by Karl Lagerfeld and Stella McCartney, among others. It appears regularly on popular name lists.

Christine, Christina
Cristín, Cristíona

Christine is a French version of the Latin name Christian, meaning 'follower of Christ'. Varying forms can be found throughout the Christian world.

Ciara
Kiera

Ciara is the female form of Ciarán. It means 'dark one' or 'black', implying dark eyes and hair. St Ciara (d 679) lived at Kilkeary, near Nenagh, Co. Tipperary. In one story, her friend St Brendan asked for her help in extinguishing a fire that burned out of control and threatened to destroy his monastery and all the surrounding land. St Ciara said one prayer and the fire was put out. It has recently become popular in the UK as well as Ireland.

Clare, Claire, Clara

Clare is Latin and means 'bright' or 'clear'. St Clare (d 1253) was very impressed with St Francis of Assisi. With his help, she formed her own community, now known as the Poor Clares. St Clare became the patron saint of television in the 20th century. The use of the additional 'i' in the name tends to be more common outside Ireland.

Clíona, Clíodhna

The meaning of the name Clíona is disputed, but some say it is taken from 'clodhna' meaning 'shapely'. In ancient Irish mythology, Clíona was a beautiful goddess who lived in the magical land of Tír Tairngire. The mortal Ciabhan persuaded her to go with him to Ireland, but while he was away hunting, Clíona, asleep on the beach, was drowned by a tidal wave. Clíona is also known as the queen of the fairies of Munster, and has a reputation for stealing young boys from fairs!

Clodagh

Clodagh is the name of two Irish rivers. Place and river names such as Clydagh, Claudy and Clady are derived from Clodagh, which means 'the clean one'. Lady Clodagh Beresford (b 1875), the daughter of the Marquis of Waterford, may have been the first person to use the name Clodagh. She was named after the river in Tipperary.

Colette, Collette

Colette is derived from Nicole, a French female pet form of Nicholas. Nicholas is Greek and means 'victory of the people'. St Colette (1381–1447) was a Franciscan hermit. She had a vision of St Francis of Assisi, who asked her to reform the Poor Clare nuns. The Avignon pope, Pedro de Luna, gave her permission to do this and she spent the rest of her life bringing convents back to the original strict rules, as well as founding 17 new houses in France and Flanders.

Colleen
Cailín

Even though Colleen comes from the Irish word meaning 'girl', it is mostly used in North America and Australia, and hardly ever in Ireland. It remains popular as a way of highlighting Irish connections in the family history.

 Courtney

Courtney is a place name that was originally used as a surname and in the 20th century began to be used as a first name. It is sometimes wrongly thought to come from the French for 'short nose', but in fact it is Norman French for 'the domain of Curtius'.

Danielle

Danielle is the female version of Daniel, a Hebrew name meaning 'God is my judge'.

Darina
Dáiríne

Darina means 'fertile', 'fruitful' or 'bountiful'. In Irish legend, Dáiríne was a princess, the younger daughter of Tuathal Teachtmar. She married Eochaid, king of Leinster, when he deceitfully told her his wife, Dáiríne's older sister Fithir, had died. But Fithir was alive, and when the sisters found out what had happened, they both died of shame and grief. Darina Allen is one of Ireland's best-known chefs.

Deborah

Deborah is Hebrew, and means 'a bee' – someone with a busy nature who seeks out the sweet aspects of life. In the Bible, Deborah was a prophet and judge of Israel. The name was brought to Ireland as an Anglicised version of the native name Gobnait [see Gobnait].

Deirdre

It is not clear what Deirdre means, though it has been given the meanings 'chatterer', 'sorrow' and 'woman'. Deirdre is the tragic heroine of a very beautiful ancient Irish story, one of the *Three Sorrows of Storytelling*. The legend was embellished by WB Yeats in *Deirdre* (1907) and by JM Synge (*Deirdre of the Sorrows*, 1910). It is one of Ireland's most popular names.

Dervla
Dearbhaile, Deirbhile

Dervla means 'daughter of Fal' – Fal is a poetic name for Ireland. Others suggest a derivation from dearbhail, meaning 'true'. St Deirbhile founded a convent at Fal Mór, Co. Mayo, in the 6th century.

Diana

Diana is Latin and means 'goddess'. Diana was the Roman goddess of the moon and of hunting. She was the equivalent of the Greek goddess Artemis, known for her beauty and chastity. Diana, Princess of Wales (1961–97), made the name very popular in the late 20th century.

Dorothy
Doireann

Doireann seems to be connected with a word meaning 'an oak grove'. The Anglicised Dorothy comes from Greek and means 'the gift of God'. There are several women in Irish myth and legend called Doireann. One was a fairy woman, daughter of Bodb, who plagued Fionn Mac Cumhaill to marry her. He refused, so she gave him a cup of enchanted mead that sent him mad. There is some disagreement among scholars as to whether Doireann actually translates as Dorothy or not.

Dymphna
Dympna

If Dymphna is Irish and a version of the name Damhnait, it could mean 'one fit to be', or possibly 'a fawn'. St Dymphna, according to legend, was an Irish princess who, to avoid the amorous advances of her father after her mother died, fled to Gheel, near Antwerp, in Flanders. St Dymphna is the patron saint of epileptics and the insane. Dympna and the variant Devnet are still in use.

Éadaoin, Étáin

Étáin may be the name of the ancient Celtic sun goddess, derived from a word that means 'jealousy'. There are a few saints named Étáin. It is Anglicised to Aideen [see Aideen]. One Étáin, knowing that the father of her baby, Art, son of Conn of the Hundred Battles, had died in battle, journeyed to his friend Lugna in Connacht. On the way, she went into labour. A she-wolf took the baby off to its lair and suckled him. Étáin finally reached Lugna and one of his retainers found the baby crawling about. He was named Cormac Mac Airt.

Eileen, Aileen
Eibhlín

Eileen probably comes from the Norman-French Aveline (which also gives the name Evelyn), though some scholars believe it is an Irish form of Helen [see Helen]. Eibhlín Caomhánach was the daughter of a chief. She is thought by many to have been the inspiration for the love ballad *Eibhlín a Rúin* (Eileen Aroon) attributed to Cearbhall Ó Dálaigh (around 1590–1630) and still a popular song at weddings.

Eithne, Ethna

Eithne means 'kernel'. The name Eithne appears often in ancient Irish myth and legend. There are also at least nine saints called Eithne. Eithne, daughter of Balor, king of the Fomorians, was the mother of Lug Lámfhota. Eithne, as a bride, was stolen from her husband by Finnbheara, king of the Connacht fairies. To get her back, her husband had to dig a hole deep enough to let light into Finnbheara's realm. But each night the hole filled up, until he was advised to sprinkle the soil with salt and Eithne was returned. Anglicised as Annie and currently still popular as such. Eithne is the given name of the popular musician Enya.

Elaine

Elaine is a French version of Helen [see Helen]. There are several women called Elaine in the stories about King Arthur and his knights. Elaine of Benoic was the wife of King Ban and the mother of Sir Lancelot. The child was stolen by the Lady of the Lake, who raised Lancelot. Elaine did not see him again until just before she died. Elaine of Carbonek used magic to trick Sir Lancelot, and became the mother of Sir Galahad.

Eleanor
Eileanóir, Eileanóra

Eleanor comes from the Provençal name Aliénor. Many scholars think it is a version of Helen [see Helen], but others think it may be German in origin, and mean 'foreign'. Eleanor of Aquitaine (around 1122–1204) was married to Louis VII of France, then to Henry II of England. The name has many variant spellings, one of which may be the Irish martyr, St Ealanor. Eleanor MvEvoy is a well-known Irish singer-songwriter.

Elizabeth
Eilís

Elizabeth is Hebrew and means 'God is my oath' or 'My God is satisfaction'. In the Bible, Elisabeth was the mother of St John the Baptist, and the Virgin Mary's cousin. She is considered a saint, one of several saints called Elizabeth. Isabel is another version of this name [see Isabel], from which the name came to Ireland in the Middle Ages. The version spelt using 'z' is most common in England (possibly thanks to the regal use of the name) while the 's' spelling is most often found in continental Europe, based on the Biblical spelling.

Emer, Éimear

Scholars do not know what the name Emer means. Emer was the wife of the great hero Cúchulainn. She had all six gifts of women: beauty, chastity, a gentle voice, sweet speech, skill in needlework and wisdom. The name has seen a renewal in popularity with the resurgent interest in Gaelic. In 1921 WB Yeats chronicalised the myth in *The Only Jealousy of Emer*.

Emily
Eimíle

Emily comes from the Latin family name Aemilius, which probably means 'rival'. Emily Brontë (1818–48), the poet and author of *Wuthering Heights*, was of Irish extraction. The name is said to have come to Ireland from England.

Emma

Emma is old German and means 'whole' or 'universal' and can also mean 'strong'. Emma of Normandy (d 1052) was the second wife of Ethelred II of England. Emma's son by her first marriage came to the throne as Edward the Confessor. The name has a strong literary connection, notably Emma Bovary in Gustave Flaubert's *Madame Bovary* and Emma Woodhouse in Jane Austen's *Emma*. One of the most popular names in Ireland for many years, despite its lack of Gaelicism.

Enya

Enya is the version of Eithne used in Donegal [see Eithne]. Enya is the name used by Eithne Ní Bhraonáin, the Grammy award-winning and internationally popular singer and composer. Enya was born in Co. Donegal, and is a member of the Brennans, a well-known musical family. She has worked with the family folk band Clannad and is Ireland's bestselling solo musician.

Erin

Éirinn, meaning 'Ireland', is the dative form of Eire. In ancient Irish legend, three divine sisters, Eriu, Banba and Fódla, met the Milesian invaders. Each wanted the invaders to name the country after herself. Eriu won, although the names of her sisters are also used for Ireland in poetry. Eriu becomes Eire in modern Irish and Erin is the Anglicised version. It is gaining in popularity worldwide.

Esther

Esther may be a Persian translation of 'Hadassah' – 'myrtle' – a Hebrew name, or it may be from the Persian word 'stara', meaning 'star'. In the Bible, Esther was a beautiful Jewish captive, who married the Persian king Ahasuerus. When she discovered that the king's counsellor, Haman, was planning to massacre the Jews, Esther managed to expose the plot and save her people. Its harmony with 'Easter' has led to many children born at this time being given the name of Esther.

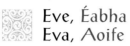

Eve, Éabha
Eva, Aoife

Eve comes from a Hebrew word and means 'life' or 'living'. In the Bible Eve was the first woman. God made her to be a companion for Adam in the Garden of Eden and Adam named her. The Irish form Eabha has seen a renewal of popularity in recent years. Eva is an Anglicisation of the traditional name Aoife.

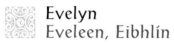

Evelyn
Eveleen, Eibhlín

Evelyn comes from the same root as Eileen [see Eileen]. Eibhlín Dubh Ní Chonaill (18th century) wrote the intensely moving poem *The Lament for Art O'Leary* in memory of her dead husband.

Fidelma

The ancient Irish meaning of Fidelma is not known, though later it was taken to mean 'faithful Mary'. There are several women in ancient Irish legend and history called Fidelma (often spelled Fedelm or Fedelma) including some saints. Fedelm was a prophetess who told Queen Medb of Connacht that her war with Ulster would fail. One of Conchobar Mac Nessa's daughters was a beautiful warrior, Fedelm Noichrothach.

Fiona
Fíona, Fíne

Fiona seems to have been based on the word fionn, meaning 'white' or 'fair'. Fiona is a fairly modern, invented name. It was first used by the Scottish poet James Macpherson (1736–96) in a series of poems about the heroes Fingal and Ossian, which he said were translated from Gaelic, but most of which he had written himself.

Fionnuala, Finola

In ancient Irish legend, Finnguala was one of the four children of Lir, transformed into swans by a jealous stepmother and condemned to keep that form for 900 years. The popular short version, Nuala, is sometimes used for the name of the queen of the fairies. Fionnuala means 'white shoulders'. The name is back in fashion after a fall from grace and the more common usage of the Anglicised versions Flora and Penelope in the 20th century.

Frances
Proinnsias, Próinséas

Frances is the female version of Francis, a Germanic name meaning 'free' or 'French'. Mrs Cecil Frances Alexander (1818–95), the wife of the Archbishop of Armagh, wrote hymns for children. Many are still used, including 'Once in Royal David's City' and 'All Things Bright and Beautiful'. Its pet form, Fanny, is sometimes used as an independent name. Fanny Parnell (1848–1882) ran the Women's Land League with her sister Anna when their brother, Charles Stewart Parnell, was in prison. European forms include Francesca and Françoise.

Gemma

Gemma is the Italian word for 'gem', 'jewel'. St Gemma Galgani (1878–1903) wanted to be a nun, but was prevented by spinal tuberculosis. She was intensely religious and for some while, stigmata – the marks of the crucifixion – appeared on her hands and feet. She had ecstasies and visions which contrasted with the patience with which she bore her ill-health and her quiet life.

Gillian

The names Gillian and Julian come from the Roman family name Julius, most famously borne by Gaius Julius Caesar. Gillian is now the female version of Julian, a name used for men and women until the 17th century, when the spelling Gillian was used to differentiate the sexes. It is attributed with the meaning 'young nestling'.

Gobnait

Gobnait was the name of the 6th-century Irish abbess who became Saint Gobnait of Ballyvourney. Her feast day is celebrated on 11 February.

Grace, Grania
Gráinne

Grace comes from Latin word 'gratia', meaning 'grace'. It is used to Anglicise Grania. Gráinne means 'she who inspires terror'. In Irish legend, Gráinne was the daughter of Cormac Mac Airt, promised in marriage to the ageing Fionn Mac Cumhaill. Instead, she fell in love and eloped with Fionn's nephew, Diarmait Ua Duibne. Gráinne Mhaol Ní Mháille – Grace O'Malley – (around 1530–1603) was a famous pirate whose base was Clare Island and the Mayo coast. Many legends have formed about her.

Hanna, Hannah

Hannah is Hebrew and means 'He [God] has favoured me'. In the Bible, Hannah was the wife of Elkanah. Desperately wanting a child, she prayed for a son she could dedicate to God's service. Her prayers were answered, and she gave birth to the prophet Samuel. Hanna Sheehy-Skeffington (1877–1946) was a co-founder of the Irish Women's Franchise League and a founder member of the Irish Women Workers Union. The name has enjoyed a huge upsurge in popularity recently.

Heather

Heather is one of the plant and flower names that became popular at the end of the 19th century. It is the name of a member of the Heath family, a low-growing hardy plant with purple or white flowers. Its popularity in Celtic countries may be attributed to the fact that it grows all over the countryside.

Helen

Helen is a Greek name meaning 'bright one' or 'radiant'. In Greek legend, Helen was the beautiful wife of Menelaus, king of Sparta. She ran off with Paris, which sparked the Trojan War. St Helen (around 255–330) was the British wife of the Roman emperor Constantius Chlorus, and the mother of the emperor Constantine. She became a Christian and visited the Holy Land where she helped the poor. The name has many derivatives [see also Elaine, Eileen, Eleanor].

Holly
Cuileann

Holly has been used as a girl's name since the beginning of the 20th century, when it was fashionable to choose botanical names for christening children. Holly is an evergreen shrub or tree, a member of the Ilex family. In ancient Ireland, holly trees were held in high regard. They were thought to protect people from evil influences. In Christian times, holly has been considered a lucky tree, particularly associated with Christmas, though the thorns and red berries look ahead to Christ's passion at Easter. St Ronan planted holly around his cell in Brittany as a safeguard against evil.

Ida, Ita
Íde

Ida comes from a Germanic word meaning 'work'. There may also be references to Mount Ida in Crete, birthplace of Zeus, the king of the gods in classical mythology. Ita comes from an old Irish word and means 'thirst', as in the thirst for knowledge. Ita is Anglicised as Ida. St Ita (around 570) was the abbess of a convent at Killeedy in Co. Limerick. Here she ran a school for small boys, one of whom may have been St Brendan. There are many legends about St Ita. There is a whitethorn tree at Killeedy said to have grown from a thorn she took from the hoof of her donkey. In legend she is none other than the foster mother of Jesus.

Imelda

Imelda is Italian or Spanish, taken from a German name meaning 'universal battle'. Imelda Marcos was the wife of Ferdinand Marcos, 10th president of the Philippines. She had a very extravagant lifestyle, and when her husband was overthrown, she was found to own 15 mink coats, 888 handbags and over 1,000 pairs of shoes.

Isabel, Isobel
Isibéal, Sibéal

Isabel is the Spanish version of Elizabeth [see Elizabeth]. St Isabel of Portugal (1271–1336) was the wife of King Dennis. She founded a hospital, a rescue home for women and an orphanage, but died after following the Portuguese army in the field trying to stop a war between her son King Alfonso IV and the king of Castile. Isabella Augusta, Lady Gregory (1852–1932), was a playwright and folklorist, who worked with WB Yeats to create the Irish National Theatre, The Abbey.

Iseult

Iseult was an Irish princess, promised in marriage to King Mark of Cornwall. Tristram, one of the Knights of the Round Table, was sent to escort Iseult to Cornwall, but on the voyage the pair were enchanted and fell in love. After many adventures, Tristram married Iseult of Brittany. The tale was made more famous in Wagnerian opera. Iseult is Cornish or Welsh, and means 'fair to look on'. The name is still used in modern times, as well as its variations, Isolda, Yseult, Ysolte.

Jacinta

Jacinta is the Spanish form of Hyacinth and the name of a precious stone. In the Book of Revelation in the Bible, the 11th stone that garnished the walls of the heavenly city was a jacinth. The jewel name jacinth comes from the Greek flower name, hyacinth. The hyacinth flower – a dark lily, not the modern hyacinth – sprang from the blood of a young man called Hyacinth, accidentally killed by the god Apollo.

Jacqueline

Jacqueline is French, a female pet version of Jacques, the French for James, meaning 'supplanter'. Soeur Jacqueline Pascal (1625–61) was a nun, and the sister of Blaise Pascal, the French mathematician, physicist and theologian. The name was hugely popular in the 1960s because of the fame of Jacqueline Kennedy, wife of US president, John F Kennedy.

Jane
Síne

Jane is the modern form of Joan, a female version of John, meaning 'Jehovah has been gracious'. Jane Francesca, Lady Wilde (1826–96) was a poet, journalist (often working under the name Speranza) and folklorist. She was the mother of Oscar Wilde. *Jane Eyre* is an enduringly popular novel by Charlotte Brontë. For a short time, it was popular when teamed with another name, as in Mary-Jane, Sarah-Jane.

Janet
Sinéad

Janet is a version of Jane, particularly popular in Scotland. Sinéad is the Irish form of Janet [see Jane, Sinéad]. Janet Gordon was the pen name of the eminent Irish historian Cecil Woodham-Smith (1896–1977), a member of the FitzGerald family. Under her own name her histories included *The Great Hunger*, a classic account of the Irish famine.

Jean

Jean is a female form of Jehanne, a French version of John, meaning 'Jehovah has been gracious'.

Jennifer

Jennifer is the Cornish form of Guinevere. Guinevere comes from two Welsh words and means 'white', 'fair' or 'smooth'. In the stories of King Arthur, Guinevere was his queen, but she loved Sir Lancelot and he loved her. This relationship was one of the causes of the downfall of the Round Table and King Arthur.

Jessica

 Jessica may come from the Hebrew 'Yiscah', which means 'God is looking'. Jessica is a comparatively modern name: it first appears in Shakespeare's play *The Merchant of Venice* as the name of Shylock's daughter. Shakespeare may have used the biblical name Yiscah for his character – in the Bible that Shakespeare knew, it was spelled Jesca.

Joan
Siobhán, Siún

Joan is a female version of John, via the French Jehanne. John is Hebrew, meaning 'Jehovah has been gracious'. St Joan of Arc (d 1431) was a peasant girl who heard 'voices' telling her to save France from the invading English. The dauphin gave her armour and men, the French forces were victorious and the dauphin was crowned King Charles VII. Joan was captured, sold to the English, found guilty on charges of witchcraft and heresy and burned at the stake. Joan Denise Moriarty (1912–92) was the founder of a ballet school and corps de ballet that became the Irish National Ballet in 1971.

Joanna

 Joanna is a version of John, meaning 'Jehovah has been gracious'. According to St Luke, one of the ancestors of Jesus was called Joanna. Another Joanna was the wife of Herod's steward, Chuza. Jesus cured her of a disease, and she was one of a group of women who helped look after him and the disciples. The name came to Ireland with the Anglo-Normans and was Gaelicised as Siobhán [see Siobhán, Joan].

Josephine
Seosaimhín

Josephine is a female version of Joseph, which is Hebrew, meaning 'God shall add'. Josephine Beauharnais (1763–1814) was an aristocrat who escaped the guillotine during the French Revolution, though her husband was executed. The widow then married Napoleon Bonaparte, becoming Empress of France. Divorced in 1809, she retired to her house, Malmaison, and grew roses.

Judith

Judith is Hebrew and means 'Jewess' or 'woman from Judah'.
A story in the Apocrypha tells how the Assyrians invaded Israel and
besieged Bethulia. Judith, a beautiful Bethulian widow, tricked the Assyrian
commander Holofernes and beheaded him in his sleep. The Assyrians were
totally demoralised and quickly driven out of Israel. Judy Garland (1922–69)
was a film actress and singer who claimed Irish and Scottish descent. She
starred in *The Wizard of Oz* in 1939, at the age of 17.

Julia, Julie
Síle

Julia is the female version of Julius, a Roman family name most famously
borne by Gaius Julius Caesar. It has been used to Anglicise the Gaelic Síle
[see Sheila]. Julia Grenan was a despatch carrier during the Easter Rising,
one of the three women who stayed in the General Post Office until the
end and who were the last to come out.

Karen
Caireann

Karen, derived from Catherine, comes from a Greek word meaning 'pure'.
Caireann comes from the Latin word carina, meaning 'beloved'. Karen is
the Danish form of Catherine or Katherine, taken to America by migrants.
It has only been used since the 1940s in Ireland and Britain. Caireann,
sometimes Anglicised as Karen, was the name of Cairenn Casdubh, a
British princess and second wife of Eochaid Mugmedón. Eochaid's jealous
first wife treated Cairenn like a slave. Cairenn's baby was born by the well
and taken by the poet Torna, who fostered him. The baby grew to be Niall
Noígíallach, or Niall of the Nine Hostages [see Niall].

Kayleigh, Kayley

The name Kayleigh could be made up of the names Kay and Leigh.
Kay is Scottish Gaelic, and means 'giant', and Leigh is old English, meaning
'field' or 'meadow'. Kayleigh is a modern name with possible roots as a
surname. It might also include a reference to Cael, which means 'slender'.
Cael was a hero of the Fianna who loved the fairy Cred. When Cael died,
Cred lay down in his grave beside him and died.

Keelin
Caoilfhionn

Keelin is the Anglicised spelling of Caoilfhionn, which means 'slender and fair'. St Caoilfhionn was a daughter of Fergus Mac Ross and a pious nun. She was known for her sweet temper, but little else!

Kelly

Kelly may be a version of the Irish name Ceallach. Ceallach may mean 'bright-headed' or 'strife'. Kelly was originally a surname derived from cill, the Irish for 'church'. It has only been used as a female name recently. Ceallach Cualand was the father of St Mungo (also known as St Kentigern).

Kerry

Kerry is the name of an Irish county. It was originally used as a first name in Australia and is now popular amongst Irish-Americans. Kerry probably comes from 'ciar', meaning 'dark'.

Laoise
This name is derived from the male form Laoiseach. It may be connected to the sun god Lugh, or simply mean 'from Laois'.

Laura
Laura is the female version of Laurus, a Latin name meaning 'laurel'. It may have links with the crown of laurels, a sign of victory or excellence. St Laura (d 864) was born in Cordoba, Spain. After she was widowed, she entered a convent at Cuteclara. She was captured by the Moors who scalded her to death by throwing her in a vat of molten lead. Laura is currently a popular name in Ireland.

Lauren
Lauren seems to be a female version of Laurence, meaning 'from Laurentium'. Lauren Bacall (1924–2014) was an American film and stage actress who was married to the actor Humphrey Bogart. The name has recently seen an upsurge in popularity in Ireland.

Leah

Leah is Hebrew. It probably means 'languid' or 'weary', but it could mean 'wild cow'. In the Bible, Leah was the first wife of Jacob. Jacob had agreed to serve Leah's father, Laban, for seven years in order to marry Leah's sister Rachel, but when the time was up, he was tricked into marrying Leah, the elder sister. Jacob had to serve another seven years for Rachel. It has appeared on top 20 naming lists for many years.

Leanne

Leanne is a modern name. It is not very clear where it comes from. It could be the names Lee and Ann joined together [see Lee and Ann]. It could be a different spelling of the name Liane or Lianna, which may come from the old Roman family name Aelidnus. Another possibility is that it comes from the Gaelic word leannán, which means 'sweetheart'.

Líadain

Líadain was a 7th-century nun who lived in Kerry. She met the poet Cuirithir and they fell in love. However, such a love was forbidden. Cuirithir became a monk and moved to a different part of Ireland. When he heard that Líadain was going to visit him, Cuirithir sailed away in a coracle and never returned. Líadain went to a stone where Cuirithir used to pray and waited for him there until she died. Líadain means 'grey lady'.

Lily, Lilly, Lelia

Lily is a flower name, one of the plant names that became popular at the end of the 19th century. A lily is a symbol of purity. Lily O'Brien's is the name of one of Ireland's top chocolate companies and is named after the founder's daughter.

Lisa

Lisa is a pet form of Elizabeth [see Elizabeth]. Lisa Gherardini (1479–1542) married the wealthy Florentine businessman Francesco del Giocondo in 1495. Well-born Florentine ladies were addressed as Mona, a shortened form of Madonna, meaning 'my lady'. Her husband commissioned a portrait of Lisa from Leonardo da Vinci, which was started in 1502. This picture, now known as the *Mona Lisa* or *La Gioconda*, is one of the most famous in the world and is in the Louvre Museum in Paris.

Louise

Louise is the female version of Louis or Lewis, a Germanic name meaning 'famous warrior'. St Louise de Marillac (1591–1660) was a supporter of St Vincent de Paul and helped him found the Daughters of Charity.

Lucy
Loiseach, Luighseach

Lucy comes from the old Roman male personal name Lucius, which means 'light'. St Lucy (d 304) was martyred at Syracuse in Sicily. She is said to have been blinded, and consequently became the patron saint of those suffering from eye diseases. Luighseach seems to mean 'bright girl'. St Luighseach was one of the early virgin saints.

Madeleine, Madelyn

 St Madeleine Sophie (1779–1865) wanted to be a Carmelite lay sister. However, she was asked by the superior of the Sacred Heart Fathers to take charge of a school in Amiens in France. This was the first house of the Society of the Sacred Heart for girls' education. By the time St Madeleine died, the Society had spread to 12 countries in Europe, and to the USA, and was one of the best educational organisations the Roman Catholic church had. Madeleine is the French version of the place name given to a woman in the Bible: Mary Magdalene, or Mary of Magdala. Magdala was a village on the Sea of Galilee.

Maeve
Méabh, Meadhbh, Medb

Maeve means 'intoxicating' or 'she who makes drunk'. There were two important characters called Maeve in ancient Irish myth and legend. Medb Lethderg was the goddess of sovereignty at Tara. She was married to nine successive kings of Ireland. Medb was the fierce warrior-queen of Connacht whose exploits are related in the epic *Táin Bó Cúailnge*: her raid on Ulster to capture the brown bull of Cooley was repelled by the hero Cúchulainn. Medb also appeared as a minor character in other stories. Maeve Binchy (1940–2012) was a popular Irish novelist and newspaper columnist.

Margaret
Máiréad

Margaret comes from a Greek word, and means 'a pearl'. Margaret Cousins (1878–1954) was a co-founder of the Irish Women's Franchise League. Máiréad Ni Ghráda (1896–1971) was a poet, writer and broadcaster. Her play *An Triail* is one of the most successful ever written in Irish. Máiréad Corrigan was the co-founder, with Betty Williams, of the Community of Peace People, an organisation that tried to find a peaceful solution to the troubles in Northern Ireland. They received the Nobel Prize for Peace in 1976, and Máiréad was awarded the Pacem in Terris Award in 1990.

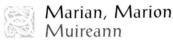

Marian, Marion
Muireann

Marian is a French pet form of Mary [see Mary]. Muireann is Irish and means either 'white sea' or 'white neck'. In ancient legend, Muirenn was the wife of Cumhall and mother of Fionn. Muirenn gave birth to her baby after Cumhall was killed by his enemies, but gave the baby to her sister, the druidess Bodhmall, and her friend Liath Luachra to bring up. Marian Finucane is a popular Irish broadcaster.

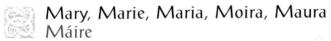

Mary, Marie, Maria, Moira, Maura
Máire

Some scholars think Mary, which is Hebrew, means 'bitterness'. Others think it means 'star of the sea'. Mary is the same name as Miriam, and there are several Marys and Miriams in the Bible, most importantly, Mary the mother of Jesus. Máire Mhac an tSaoi – Maire Cruise O'Brien – is an Irish language scholar, poet and diplomat. Mary Robinson is a lawyer who became President of Ireland in 1990. Mary McAleese is a barrister and academic, and a former two-term President of Ireland, first elected in 1997. Mary has been a popular girl's name in Ireland for many years.

Maureen
Máirín

Maureen is the Anglicised spelling of the Irish Máirín, which means 'little Mary' [see Mary]. Maureen O'Hara (1920–2015) was an Irish film actor and singer who worked with such actors as Charles Laughton and John Wayne and the director John Ford. She spoke fluent Irish, which she used in films.

Megan

Megan is a Welsh pet form of Margaret [see Margaret].

Melissa

Melissa is Greek and means 'bee'. In Greek mythology, Melissa was a brave and helpful nymph. Zeus's father Cronos had been told he would be deposed by one of his children, so, as they were born, he ate them. When Zeus was born, his mother Rhea tricked Cronos by giving him a stone wrapped in baby clothes to eat. Zeus was hidden and fed on milk and honey by Melissa. When Cronos discovered the trick, he turned Melissa into a worm, but grateful Zeus changed her into a queen bee.

Mella

Mella means 'lightning'. Legend says that Mella was the sister of St Kevin of Glendalough, and the mother of seven saints. Justice Mella Carroll (1935–2006) was Ireland's first female high court judge.

Michelle

Michelle is the female form of Michel, the French version of Michael. This is a Hebrew name, meaning 'who is like God?'

Molly

Molly is a pet form of Mary [see Mary]. Molly Maguire was supposed to have been an Irish widow who refused to be ejected from her cottage by the agents of an English landlord. Her name was used by a secret society of rebels in the late 18th and early 19th centuries, at a time of rural unrest in Ireland. Molly Keane (1904–96) was a Kildare-born novelist who was a member of Aosdána, the Irish association of people in the arts. Molly Malone is one of Dublin's most famous characters.

Mona

Mona was the name given by the Romans to an area of the west coast of Britain, including the islands. Mon is the Welsh name for Anglesey, and Man is known as Mona's Isle. Some scholars think it may come from the Greek monos, meaning 'single', but most think it is a pet name taken from the Irish 'muadhnait', meaning 'noble' or 'little noble one'.

Natasha

Natasha is a pet form of the name Natalya, which is Russian and means 'Christmas'. It is a popular name for girls born around 25th December. Natalie is another variant from the same root, being French in origin.

Nessa
Neasa

Nessa means 'ungentle'. It can also be a pet form of the names Agnes and Vanessa [see Vanessa]. In ancient Irish legend, Nessa was the daughter of Eochaid Sálbuide, and the mother of Conchobar Mac Nessa. When Fergus Mac Róich was about to become king of Ulster, Nessa tricked him into letting Conchobar reign for a year. Fergus agreed, but at the end of the year Nessa made it so difficult for him to take up the kingship that he departed. Conchobar ruled well, guided by Nessa.

Niamh

Niamh means 'brightness' or 'radiance'. In Irish legend, Niamh was the beautiful girl loved by Oisín, son of Fionn Mac Cumhaill. In the earliest stories Niamh was mortal and took Oisín to Ulster, where she came from. A later and more famous version had Niamh Chinn Óir taking Oisín to the magical country of Tír na nÓg. He thought he had spent a day with her, but in fact 300 years had passed.

Nicola, Nichola, Nicole
Nicola is the female version of Nicholas, which is Greek and means 'victory of the people'.

Nollaig
Nollaig is the Irish word for Christmas and often given to girls born around 25 December.

Nora
Nóra
Nora was originally short for names such as Eleanora, Honora and Leonora, but for many years has been used independently. Eleanor means 'foreign' and so does Leonora, which is another version of the name. Honora means 'honour'. Nora Barnacle (1884–1951) was the mistress and later the wife of James Joyce. Nora Connolly O'Brien (1893–1981) was the daughter of James Connolly. She was involved in the Howth gun-running in 1914, and founded the Young Republican party. Norah McGuinness (1901–80) was an artist who co-founded and was second president of the Irish Exhibition of Living Art. Reportedly, the name was so widespread in Medieval Ireland that people mistakenly took the name to be Irish.

Noreen
Nóirín
Noreen is the Anglicised spelling of the Irish pet form of Nora [see Nora].

Nuala
Fionnuala
Nuala is a shortened form of Fionnuala, now used independently. In full, the name means 'white shoulders'. It was very popular until quite recently.

Olivia

Olivia is a female form of Oliver, from the Latin plant name meaning 'olive'. It has obvious links with the olive branch of peace. There are three saints called Olivia, though little is known of them. St Olivia of Brescia (d 138) was martyred during the emperor Hadrian's persecution and her remains are still in St Afra's church in Brescia, Italy.

Orla
Orlaith, Orlagh

Orla means 'golden princess'. It was an immensely popular name in medieval Ireland. Orla was the name of a sister of the high king Brian Bórama, and also the name of his niece.

Orna

Orna means 'dun' or 'sallow'. Orna is the female version of Orán or Odhdrán, the name of at least 20 saints. Orna was the wife of Guaire, king of Connacht, who built the castle of Dunguaire at Kinvarra.

Pamela

Pamela is a name invented in 1590 by the writer Sir Philip Sidney for a character in his romance *Arcadia* and appears later in literature as the title character in Samuel Richardson's 1740 novel. It means 'honey' and suggests a person of great sweetness.

Patricia

Patricia is the female version of Patrick, which is from Latin and means 'patrician' or 'of noble birth'. The name has a long history, much of it in Scotland, but seems popular in Ireland in modern times thanks to the association of the patron saint. Patricia Lynch (1898–1972) was a popular children's author who often used Irish folktales, history and magic as the background for her stories, and was influenced by the seanchaí (professional storytellers) she had heard as a girl in Cork.

Paula, Pauline
Póilín

Paula is the female version of Paul, a Latin word meaning 'small'. St Paula (347–404) was a rich and well-connected Roman who built houses for the followers of St Jerome, and a hospice for pilgrims. Póilín is comparatively new but is becoming popular.

Philippa

Philippa is the female version of Philip, which is Greek and means 'lover of horses'. Philippa of Hainault (around 1314–69) was a Flemish princess who married King Edward III of England. The shortened form Pippa is also a name in its own right.

Philomena

Philomena is Greek and means 'love and strength' or 'loving strength'. Philomena was thought to be a saint's name and its popularity rose. However, a ruling by the Catholic church – dropping the name from the liturgical calendar of saints – changed its fortunes and the name is now less commonly found.

Rachel, Rachael

Rachel is Hebrew and means 'ewe' or 'lamb'. In the Bible, Rachel became the second wife of Jacob. It has featured in top-ten lists for several years.

Rebecca, Rebekah

Rebecca is probably Aramaic, and might mean 'heifer' or 'captivator', but scholars are uncertain. In the Bible, Rebecca was the wife of the patriarch Isaac, and the mother of Jacob and Esau. This is another name with long-standing presence in the top 50 in Ireland.

Regina
Ríoghnach, Ríonach

Both the Latin Regina and the Irish Ríonach mean 'queen'. Regina as a name usually refers to the Latin phrase 'regina coeli', meaning Queen of Heaven, one of the titles of the Virgin Mary. Ríonach was the wife of Niall Noígíallach, or Niall of the Nine Hostages. Two of her sons founded kingdoms in the north, Tír Chonaill (Donegal) and Tír Eoghain (Tyrone). There was a St Regina in the 3rd century, at Autun in France.

Robyn

Robyn used as a girl's name seems to come from the robin, the cheerful garden bird. Robin (and Robyn, the Welsh spelling) are pet forms of Robert, which is old German and means 'bright fame'.

Róisín

Róisín is a pet form of Rós, the Irish for Rose, but as it was used long before the Victorian use of flower names for girls, it may be derived from an old German word meaning 'fame'. Róisín has been used in Ireland for hundreds of years, but it is particularly associated with a personification of Ireland in *Róisín Dubh*, a 17th-century poem attributed to Owen Roe MacWard.

Rosaleen

Rosaleen is a form of Rosalyn, formed of two Frankish words meaning 'horse' and 'tender' or 'soft'. Rosaleen is a personification of Ireland in *Dark Rosaleen*, James Mangan's translation of the poem *Róisín Dubh*.

Rose
Rós, Róise

Today, Rose is usually thought to come from rosa, the Latin word for the flower. However, it is probably German in origin, meaning either 'horse' or 'fame'. St Rose of Lima (1586–1617) was the first person in the Americas to be canonised.

Rosemary

Rosemary is sometimes thought to be a combination of 'Rose' and 'Mary', with reference to the Virgin Mary. It is in fact one of the plant names that were popular at the end of the 19th century. Rosemary – the aromatic shrub – was particularly associated with remembrance. Rosemary is Latin, and means 'sea dew'.

Ruth

Scholars are unsure what the name Ruth means. It might be Hebrew for 'friend'. Others ascribe the meanings 'pity' or 'compassionate'. In the Bible, Ruth was the daughter-in-law of Naomi and the wife of rich landowner Boaz. Ruth and Boaz were the forebears of King David.

Sally, Sara, Sarah
 Sorcha

Sarah is Hebrew and means 'princess'. Sorcha is Celtic, and means 'brightness'. It is used as a Gaelic form of Sarah, but in fact there is no connection between the two names. In the Bible, Sarah was the wife of the patriarch Abraham. An angel told Abraham that Sarah would have a son, and she laughed, because she knew she was too old. But God gave her a son, Isaac. Sarah has often been the most popular name in Ireland for a girl.

Saoirse
 Given to both boys and girls, this name means 'freedom'. It has been in use since the 1920s and has become more popular in recent years.

Shannon
 Sionainn

It is thought that Shannon may mean 'old'. In ancient Irish legend Sionna was the granddaughter of the sea god Lir. She desired knowledge, but that was reserved for men. Sionna went to Connla's well, where the Salmon of Knowledge lived. Around the well grew the sacred hazel trees of poetry, science and knowledge and the salmon ate the nuts that fell in the water, so whoever ate the salmon would know everything. Sionna tried to catch the salmon, but was swept into the water and drowned. The water flowed into a river, called Shannon after Sionna. The river name is now used as a first name and seems to be especially popular in the USA.

Sharon

Sharon is Hebrew and means 'a plain'. In the Bible, Sharon is a place renowned for the beauty of its flowers. Rose of Sharon is the popular name of a yellow-flowered shrub, a member of the Hypericum family. Another rose of Sharon is a purple-flowered hibiscus. From the 20th century, Sharon has been used as a girl's first name.

Shauna, Shona

Shauna is the female version of Seán, which means 'Jehovah has been gracious'. It is a very popular Irish girl's name.

Sheena, Sheenagh
Síne

Sheena is the Anglicised spelling of Síne, the Irish form of Jane [see Jane].

Sheila, Sheelagh
Síle

Sheila or Cecilia comes from the Roman family name Caecilius, which in turn comes from a Latin word meaning 'blind'. Síle is the Irish form of Cecilia and Sheila is the Anglicised phonetic spelling of Síle. St Cecilia founded a church in Rome and later became the patron saint of musicians. Sheela na Gigs are ancient stone carvings of women that emphasise their sex. Ireland has more of them than any other country. They are said to ward off death and evil, and they may be connected to the worship of a mother goddess.

Sinéad

Sinéad is the Irish form of Janet [see Janet, Jane]. Probably the best known bearer of this name in Ireland is Sinéad O'Connor.

Siobhán
Shevaun

Siobhán McKenna (1923–86) was an outstanding Irish actress. Born in Belfast and raised in Co. Galway, she spoke fluent Irish and was awarded the gold Medal of the Eire Society of Boston for promoting Irish culture. Siobhán is the Irish version of Joan [see Joan, Joanna].

Sive
Sadbh, Sadhbh

Sive means 'sweetness'. Sadbh was a beautiful girl, transformed into a doe by the druid Fer Doirich. When Fionn Mac Cumhaill's dogs chased the doe, Fionn protected her. She turned back into a girl and he married her. But Fer Doirich again enchanted Sadbh into a doe, and she had to abandon her newborn son to follow the druid. Fionn hunted for her without success, but seven years later, he found the child under a rowan tree. He was to be the hero Oisín.

Sophie, Sophia

Sophie is Greek and means 'wisdom'. The great church of St Sophia in Constantinople (now a mosque in Istanbul) is not dedicated to a person. The dedication 'he hagia Sophia' should be translated as 'holy wisdom'. St Sophia is the patron saint of widows. Sophie appears regularly in popularity lists for naming girls.

Stephanie

Stephanie is the female version of Stephen, a Greek name meaning 'crown'.

Susan, Suzanne

Susan is Hebrew and means 'lily'. Suzanne is the French version. The story of Susanna is in the Apocrypha. Susanna refused the attentions of various Jewish elders, who then accused her of adultery. Daniel proved she was innocent and the elders were put to death.

Tara

The Irish name Tara is the Anglicised spelling of Teamhrach, genitive of Temair, meaning 'dark one'. Tara is also a Buddhist name, meaning 'star'. The Irish Tara is a hill in Meath, and was the seat of the High Kings of Ireland. Its popularity as a personal name dates from the appearance of the film *Gone With the Wind*, in which Tara is the name of the heroine's estate. In Tibetan Buddhism, Tara is the wife of Avalokitesvara, who epitomises energy, mercy and compassion.

Teresa, Theresa, Thérèse
Treasa, Toiréasa

Theresa is sometimes connected to the Greek island of Thera, but there is no real evidence for this. Teresa is the Italian and Spanish form of Theresa. Therasia was the wife of the 5th-century St Paulinus, Bishop of Nola, who had been converted by her. St Teresa of Avila (1515–82) founded convents of nuns who followed the Carmelite rule very strictly, even giving up the wearing of shoes. Tracy may be a derivative of the name.

Úna
Oonagh

Some scholars think Una is Latin, meaning 'one', but others think it might be the Irish word úna, meaning 'hunger' or 'famine', or – more likely – derived from uan, meaning 'lamb'. In Irish legend, Oonagh was the wife of Finnbheara, king of the Connacht and Irish fairies. Oonagh was described as the most beautiful of all women, with golden hair falling to the ground. She had 17 sons. Other Anglicisations include Winifred, Agnes and Unity [see Agnes].

Ursula

Ursula is a pet form of the Latin word ursa, meaning 'she-bear'. St Ursula was first recorded in Cologne on an inscription cut in the 4th or 5th century. By the 9th century, legend told of a British princess who, to avoid an unwanted marriage, went to Rome with ten companions. On the way home, they were killed by Huns at Cologne because they were Christian. Later, the number of Ursula's companions had grown to 11,000. St Ursula is the patron saint of students.

Valerie

Valerie comes from the Roman family name Valerius, meaning 'to be healthy' or 'to be strong'. St Valeria (1st century) was supposed to be the wife of St Vitalis. Her sons were St Gervasius and St Protasius, martyred at Ravenna. In France, another St Valerie was converted by St Martial, Bishop of Limoges, in the 3rd century. Taken from the French, Valerie has been popular in Ireland over the years.

Vanessa

Vanessa is a name invented by the writer and political satirist Jonathan Swift (1667–1745), Dean of St Patrick's in Dublin. He devised it for his friend Esther Vanhomrigh when he made her a character in the poem 'Cadenus and Vanessa' – it uses the first part of her surname and possibly the first syllable of her first name.

Veronica

Some scholars think Veronica is a Latin version of Berenice, which is Greek and means 'victory bringer'. Others think it is an abbreviation of the Latin 'vera iconica', meaning 'true image'. St Veronica was supposed to be the name of a woman in Jerusalem who, taking pity on Christ's suffering as he carried the cross, wiped the sweat off his face with her veil. The image of his face was then miraculously found on the cloth.

Vivienne, Bevin
Bébhinn

Vivienne is sometimes taken as the female form of Vivian, which is Latin, meaning 'full of life'. It might also be a misreading of the Gaelic name Ninian. Bébhinn means 'fair woman'. Because it sounds like Vivienne, it is often thought to be an Irish version of the name, but in fact there is no connection. In the stories of King Arthur and the Knights of the Round Table, Vivienne is a powerful, mysterious fairy. Bébhinn was a lovely giantess who asked Fionn Mac Cumhaill's Fianna to protect her from her giant husband. Sadly the giant broke into the palace and killed her.

Yvonne

Yvonne is the female, pet form of the French name Yves. This comes from a Germanic personal name, and means 'yew'. The name is fairly common in Ireland. It is sometimes shortened to Eve.

Zoe

Zoe is Greek and means 'life'. Zoe (around 978–1052) was the daughter of the Byzantine emperor Constantine VIII. She was co-ruler of the Byzantine Empire from 1028–50. Zoe had three husbands. First she married Romanos III, but he died in suspicious circumstances and on the same day Zoe married a courtier who reigned as Michael IV. They adopted a nephew, who ruled as Michael V. This emperor exiled Zoe, but the people of Byzantium forced him to bring her back and she and her sister deposed him. Finally Zoe married Constantine IX, who survived her by four years.

Adam

Patrick

Fergus

Columb

Raymond

Liam

Brendan Nial

Eanna

Barry

Stewart

James William

Aaron

Malcolm

Art

Callum

Garrett

Aaron

Aaron is the Hebrew form of a name which may originally have come from Egypt. Aaron probably means 'lofty' or 'exalted'. In the Bible, Aaron was an older brother of Moses, and the first high priest of the Israelites. In Arabic the name is Harun. Harun al-Rashid (Aaron the Just), Caliph of Baghdad (786–809), appears in some of the stories in *The Arabian Nights' Entertainments*. It is currently one of the most popular names for boys in Ireland.

Adam

Adam means 'man', derived from the Hebrew word adama, meaning 'earth' or 'red earth'. In the Bible, Adam was the first man, created by God from dust. St Adamnán, 'Little Adam', was a 7th-century abbot of Iona, famous for writing *The Life of St Columba*. Adam was the fourth most popular name in Ireland for boys born in 2006.

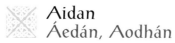

Aidan
Áedán, Aodhán

Aidan is a pet form of Aodh or Aed, meaning 'fire'. Aidan was the name of
several Irish saints, including the first bishop of Ferns, who was renowned
for his kindness, and St Aidan (d 651), a monk of Iona, who went as a
missionary to Northumberland, founding a monastery on Lindisfarne as his
headquarters. Various legends link different Aidans with a stag, and thus
the stag is often seen as a symbol of the name. The name has become
popular in the USA.

Alan
Ailin

Some scholars think the name Alan means 'rock-like' or 'steadfast', and
comes either from Scottish Gaelic ailinn or Breton alain, meaning 'rock', or
from ailill, meaning 'spirit' or 'elf'. Alan, Earl of Brittany served William the
Conqueror, and was rewarded with great estates in England. Another Alan
– better known as St Amand (d 679) – was a hermit and missionary who
became bishop of Maastricht, in the Low Countries. He is the patron saint
of brewers, innkeepers and wine merchants.

Andrew
Aindriú

Andrew comes from the Greek Andreas, and means 'strong', 'manly'
or 'courageous'. St Andrew, the first disciple to be called by Jesus, was
a fisherman from Bethsaida in Galilee. St Andrew is the patron saint of
Scotland, Greece and Russia.

Angus
Aonghus, Oengus, Aengus

Angus means 'the unique one' or 'only choice', from the Gaelic words aon meaning 'one' and gus meaning 'strength'. Aonghus Óg was the ancient Irish god of youth and love, who lived at Brugh na Bóinne (Newgrange). Another famous Aonghus was the grandson of the 10th-century Irish king, Niall Noígíollach, or Niall of the Nine Hostages.

Anthony, Antony
Antóin

Anthony is Latin and comes from the Roman family name Antonius, meaning 'priceless' or 'inestimable'. There are several saints with this name – two important ones are the Egyptian St Antony of Thebes (d 356), a hermit in the 3rd century who was the founder of Christian monasticism, and the Italian St Antony of Padua (d 1231), patron saint of the poor and of lost things.

Art

Art means 'bear' or 'champion'. It has no Celtic connection with the name Arthur, although in Anglo-Saxon it is a pet form of that name. There are several legendary heroes, including Art Mac Cuinn or Art Óenfher, son of Conn of the Hundred Battles and father of King Cormac Mac Airt, sometimes nicknamed Art the Lonely. Art won his bride Delbchaem only after a series of dangerous and exciting adventures.

Barry, Bearach

Barry means 'a spear', 'spearlike' or 'pointed'. In the 6th century, the Irish St Bearach found sites for monasteries in unusual ways. At Tara, when he was refused a drink, all the beer disappeared from the barrels. The beer only came back after the king had granted Bearach the land he wanted! He rode in a chariot pulled by a stag, and when people asked him for protection from a marauding army, Bearach turned a bog into a lake, in which the soldiers drowned.

Bartholomew, Bairtliméad, Beartlaoi

Bartholemew is from the Aramaic Bar-talmai, 'son of Talmai'. Talmai is Hebrew for 'many furrows'. In the Bible, St Bartholomew was one of the 12 disciples. Not much is known about him, but some scholars think he is the same person as the apostle Nathaniel. Parthalán is another Irish version of the Roman name Bartholomaeus.

Benedict

Benedict comes from the Latin benedictus, meaning 'blessed'. In 2005, Cardinal Joseph Ratzinger became Pope Benedict XVI. The most famous of several saints named Benedict was an Italian monk, who around 529 founded a monastery at Monte Cassino. Here he wrote a book of rules for monastic life which is still used by monks and nuns today. Benedict Kiely (1919–2007) was an Irish journalist and author who was elected Saoi of Aosdána in 1996.

Benjamin

Benjamin might mean 'son of the right hand' or 'son of (my) old age'. In the Bible, Benjamin was the 12th and last child of Jacob. His mother, Rachel, died when he was born, but not before she had named him Benoni, 'son of my sorrow'. Jacob thought this was a bad omen and renamed the baby Benjamin. Benjamin was the founder of one of the Twelve Tribes of Israel. The short version of the name, Ben, is popular in Ireland.

Bernard

Bernard comes from old German and means 'strong bear' or 'strong as a bear'. St Bernard dogs, which helped rescue Alpine travellers caught in snow, are named after St Bernard of Montjoux (923–1006). He set up rest houses where travellers could shelter in bad weather at the tops of the Great and Little St Bernard Passes. St Bernard is the patron saint of mountaineers. George Bernard Shaw (1856–1950) was born in Dublin and became a famous playwright, journalist and political campaigner. He wrote *Pygmalion*, on which the musical *My Fair Lady* was based, and is one of only two people to have been awarded both a Nobel Prize and an Oscar.

Brendan
Breandán

Brendan may come from the Gaelic bran, meaning 'raven', or the Welsh brenhyn, meaning 'prince'. Brendan the Navigator was the hero of an enormously popular medieval story. It told how St Brendan sailed to the Land of Promise, saying Mass on a whale's back and braving icebergs, volcanoes and other dangers. Some think the story is based on a very early account of a voyage to the North American continent. The real St Brendan (d 578) visited Iona, Scotland, and probably the west of Britain and Brittany. He founded the Abbey of Clonfert. Brendan is the patron saint of sailors. Brendan Behan (1923–64) was an Irish playwright and novelist.

Brian, Bryan
Briain

Some scholars think Brian comes from a Welsh or British word meaning 'high' or 'noble'. Others think it could be Breton, and mean 'dignity' or 'pride'. On Good Friday 1014, Brian Bórama (Brian Boru), the last High King of Ireland, beat the Vikings at the battle of Clontarf, ending their rule in Ireland. Brian Keenan is an Irish journalist who was held hostage in Lebanon from April 1986 to August 1990. The name has many variations and is widespread around the world in various forms, including Briano, Bryant and several surnames.

Cahal, Cathal

Cathal means 'strong battler'. Cathal Crobderg (d 1224) – Cathal of the Red Hand – was king of Connacht. His nickname came from a distinctive birthmark, which allowed him to prove his identity and claim the throne. Cathal Brugha (1874–1922) was a leader of the Easter Rising in 1916, and died in the Irish Civil War.

Calum, Callum

Calum or Callum is the Scottish Gaelic version of Columba, the Latin for 'dove' [see Colm]. It has become a popular name in recent years.

Charles

Charles comes from the German Karl or Carl, meaning 'a man'. St Charles Borromeo (1538–84) worked hard to improve the Catholic Church. He opened Sunday schools for ordinary people and seminaries for clergy. During an outbreak of plague he spent most of his money helping the sick. Charles Stewart Parnell was a 19th-century politician. Charles Haughey (1925–2006) was Taoiseach three times between 1979 and 1992.

Christopher
Críostóir

Christopher comes from the Greek Khristophorus, meaning 'bearer of Christ'. The story of the giant St Christopher, who carried the Christ-child over a dangerous river, is well known. The real St Christopher was a 3rd-century martyr about whom little is known, though he was patron saint of travellers until 1969. Christopher Columbus (1451–1506) sailed west, reaching the Bahamas in 1492, and more Caribbean islands in later years.

Cian

Cian means 'ancient'. Cian Mac Maolmhuaidhe was Brian Bórama's son-in-law. One story tells how he fell in love with a fairy woman. She turned herself into a mare, kicking Cian's leg and breaking it. No one could heal Cian until a Frenchman arrived with a magic poultice he had got from an Orkney princess. This cured the broken leg. In recent years Cian has entered the top 20 list of boy's names.

Ciarán
Kieran, Kieron

Ciarán is a pet form of 'ciar', meaning 'black'. Ciarán of Cluan left home as a boy to be trained at St Finnian's monastery. He took a dun cow with him, and the odhar Chiaráin – the dun of Ciarán – became famous. It gave him enough milk to feed the whole monastery and the countryside all around. Later, Ciarán founded one of Ireland's greatest monasteries at Clonmacnoise.

Cillian, Killian

Some scholars think the name is a pet form of 'ceallach', meaning 'strife'. Others think it comes from 'cill', meaning 'a church'. Several early Irish saints were called Cillian or Killian. One wrote *A Life of St Bridget*. Another was a missionary to Franconia, an ancient German duchy, and became an important saint in that part of Germany.

Colin
Cóilín

Colin may be a pet form of Nicholas, or a version of the Gaelic Coileán, meaning 'young hound' or 'cub'. The chief of the Scottish Clan Campbell has the title MacCailein Mór, 'son of Great Colin'.

Colm, Colum, Columb

Columba is Latin for 'dove'. Colm, Colum and Columb are all Irish versions of the name Columba. There were more than 30 saints named Columba and the most famous is Columba of Iona (d 597). Born in Donegal, he founded monasteries at Durrow, Derry and Kells, before sailing to the island of Iona in 563. From his monastery here, Columba and his monks converted Picts and Irish settlers in Scotland. *The Cathach*, the battle book of the O'Donnells, now in the Royal Irish Academy, may have been written by St Columba himself.

Colmán

Colmán is a version of Columba and means 'little dove'. Colmán was bishop of Lindisfarne (d 676). At the Synod of Whitby, which met in 664 to decide how to work out the date of Easter, Colmán argued that the Celtic method was the right one, but King Oswy of Northumberland chose the Roman way of calculating it. Colmán was so upset that he retired, settling at last on the island of Inishbofin. There are several saints with the name Colmán.

Conall
Connell

Conall means 'wolfish'. Many people in ancient Irish history and legend were called Conall. Conall Gulban, son of Niall Noígíallach, or Niall of the Nine Hostages, founded the kingdom of Tír Chonaill, now Co. Donegal. Conall Cernach was a legendary hero of the Ulster Cycle of stories, Cúchulainn's foster-brother and companion in many adventures. Conall was supposed to have swallowed an enormous boar whole!

Conán

Conán means 'hound' or 'wolf'. Conán Máel – Conán the bald – was a clownish, rather nasty member of the Fianna, the band of warriors and hunters led by the legendary Fionn Mac Cumhaill. Conán was the brother of the great Goll Mac Morna, but was a boaster and troublemaker. In some stories, Conán wears the fleece of a black sheep as a wig. Sir Arthur Conan Doyle (1859–1930) was a doctor and writer, the author of the Sherlock Holmes stories.

Conn

Some scholars think Conn means 'hound' or 'wolf'. Others think it means 'wisdom', 'chief' or 'intelligence'. Conn was a very popular name in early Irish history and legend. Conn Céadcathach – Conn of the Hundred Battles – was a legendary high king of Ireland. He is said to have reigned for over 50 years in the 2nd century BC. During his reign, Ireland enjoyed its greatest peace and prosperity: which is somewhat odd if Conn also fought 100 battles!

Conor, Connor
Conchobhar

Conor means 'lover of hounds'. Conchobar Mac Nessa was the king of Ulster in the stories of the Red Branch Knights. His most famous warrior was his foster-son, Cúchulainn. Conchobhar had the power of prophecy and owned a magic shield that screamed if anyone threatened him. Conor Cruise O'Brien (b 1917) is an historian, critic and Irish statesman. Conor is one of Ireland's most popular boys' names.

Cormac

Cormac may mean 'charioteer'. Cormac has been a popular name in Ireland since the earliest times. In the 3rd century, Cormac Mac Airt was the first High King known to have ruled from Tara. He was a wise and just king, served by Fionn Mac Cumhaill. When Cormac lost an eye in a quarrel, he had to abdicate, since a maimed man could not be High King.

 ## Daire
Dara, Daragh, Darragh

Daire means 'fruitful' or 'fertile'. Darragh can also mean 'like an oak'. Daire
was the name of many men in the legends and early history of Ireland.
One Daire was the musician of the Fianna, and another, Daire Dubh, was
a mysterious person who lived in a black tent. Daire Donn – the king of
the World – may have been a Roman emperor (or possibly Charlemagne).
Much earlier, Daire Mac Fiachna was the owner of Donn Cúailnge, the great
brown bull of Cooley, over which Cúchulainn and the Red Branch Knights
of Ulster fought a war with Queen Medb of Connacht. All four spellings are
popular to this day, with female versions Dáire and Dara also found.

Damian, Damien

Damian means 'tamer'. Some people use Damian as an Anglicised
version of Daimine, which means 'little fawn'. Damian and Cosmas were
twin brothers, both doctors, martyred during the emperor Diocletian's
persecution of Christians. The brothers did not charge fees and were called
'the holy moneyless ones'. St Damien is a patron saint of physicians. The
singer-songwriters Damien Rice and Damien Dempsey are two
well-known bearers of this name.

Daniel

Daniel is Hebrew and means 'God is my judge'. In the Bible, Daniel was one of the prophets of Israel. As a slave boy, he was able to interpret dreams, and rose to be a favoured councillor. Jealous courtiers persuaded the king to have Daniel thrown into a den of lions, but God protected him and he was not harmed.

Darren

Darren seems originally to have been a surname, used in the 20th century in the USA as a first name. From there it travelled to other countries. Darren Clarke is a golfer from Dungannon, Co. Tyrone.

David
Daibhead, Dáibhid, Dáithí

David is Hebrew and means 'beloved one' or 'darling'. David was the second king of Israel and the greatest of all Israel's kings. As a shepherd boy, he killed the Philistine giant Goliath with a shot from his sling. He was a musician, a poet and a warrior. St David (6th century) is the patron saint of Wales.

Declan
Déaglán

Declan means 'full of goodness'. St Declan was a 5th-century missionary who may have been working in Ireland before St Patrick came. Declan founded an important monastery at Ardmore, Co. Waterford. Declan Patrick MacManus is the real name of singer Elvis Costello.

Denis, Dennis

Dionysos was the Greek god of wine. Denis is a medieval version of the Greek name Dionysos. In the 3rd century St Denis (d 258) converted the Gauls. He was a bishop, martyred at the place now called Montmartre – Martyrs' Hill – in Paris. St Denis is the patron saint of France. It may also be an Anglicisation of Donagh [see Donncha].

Dermot, Dermod
Diarmaid, Diarmait, Diarmuid

Dermot may mean 'unenvious' or 'he who reverences God'. The name is very old. Diarmait Mac Murchada, a 12th-century king of Leinster, has been unpopular for centuries, because he invited the Normans into Ireland. Diarmaid Mac Aodha Sláine was High King of Ireland with his brother Bláthmac before they both died of plague in 664. Diarmaid Ó Duibhne appears in the love story *The Pursuit of Diarmaid and Gráinne* from the 9th century.

Desmond
Deasún

Desmond describes a man from south Munster (Deas Mumhan). It became the name of an area of country before counties were formed in the 17th century. The name Desmond is especially associated with the FitzGerald family, who led armed resistance to English rule, and in particular Gerald, third earl of Desmond – the Red Earl.

Dominic

Dominic is Latin and means 'belonging to the Lord'. St Dominic (d 1221) was a learned Spanish monk, who worked in southern France as a missionary and founded the Black Friars. Dominic Behan (1928–89) was a songwriter, novelist and playwright of strong Republican sympathies, somewhat overshadowed by his brother Brendan.

Dónal, Domhnall
Donald

Dónal means 'world ruler' or 'mighty ruler'. Five high kings of Ireland and three saints were called Dónal. In the spelling Donald, the name is closely associated with the Scottish clan Macdonald, the Lords of the Isles in the Middle Ages. Domhnall Ó Conaill (1775–1847) Anglicised his name to Daniel O'Connell – he was nicknamed 'the Liberator', and is remembered as Ireland's foremost politician of the early 19th century.

Donncha, Donnchadh
Donogh, Donagh, Donough

Donncha means 'brown warrior' or 'brown chief'. In about 939, the High King Donnchad commissioned a cumhdach – shrine – to preserve the precious *Book of Armagh*, which contains the only Early Irish text of the New Testament, as well as several texts about or by St Patrick. It was written around 807 and is now in the library of Trinity College, Dublin. The Irish international rugby player Donncha O'Callaghan is a modern bearer of the name.

Duane, Dwayne

Duane was originally a nickname or surname from the Irish 'dubh', meaning 'dark' or 'black'.

Dylan, Dillon

Dylan means 'son of the waves'. In the *Mabinogion*, the great sequence of ancient Welsh stories, Dylan was a sea god, the son of Arianhrod. In recent years Dylan has appeared on top-ten naming lists.

Éamon, Éamonn
Edmund

Edmund is old English and means 'rich protector'. St Edmund (841–69) was a Saxon king of East Anglia. Defeated in battle by the Danes, he refused to share his Christian kingdom, and was shot so full of arrows he looked like a thistle covered with prickles. Edmund Burke (1729–97) was a lawyer, politician and writer who championed the emancipation of Irish trade, the Irish parliament and Irish Catholics. Éamon de Valera (1882–1975) founded the Fianna Fáil party and was president of Ireland from 1959 to 1973.

Éanna, Enda

Éanna or Enda probably means 'bird-like'. In the 6th century, St Enda was given Inis Mór, the largest of the Aran Islands, by King Oengus of Muster. Here he set up Cill Éanna, the first real monastery in Ireland, 'the capital of Ireland of the saints'.

Edward

Edward is Old English and means 'rich guardian'. Lord Edward FitzGerald (1763–98) was a revolutionary who renounced his title after a visit to America. He joined the United Irishmen, plotting for a French invasion of Ireland. He was wounded while resisting arrest and died soon afterwards.

Emmet

Robert Emmet was an Irish patriot who led an unsuccessful rebellion against the British in 1798 and was sentenced to death for high treason.

Eoin
Owen

Eoin means 'young man' and was a popular name in ancient Ireland. Eoin Mac Suibhne was the chief of a band of warriors from Scotland who fought, then settled, in Donegal. Eoin Colfer (1965–) is the author of the *Artemis Fowl* stories, a very popular series of children's fantasy stories.

Eric

Eric is Norse and means 'ever ruler' or 'ever powerful'. Eric Thorvaldsson, known as Eric the Red, was a Norwegian sailor who in 995 founded Norse colonies in Greenland. St Eric became king of Sweden around 1155 and is that country's patron saint. The introduction of the name via England may have obscured the old Irish name Erc or Earc, meaning 'red' or 'speckled'.

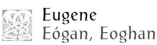

Eugene
Eógan, Eoghan

Eoghan means 'born of yew'. Eoghan was one of the two sons of Niall Noígíollach, or Niall of the Nine Hostages. He gave his name to Tír Eoghain, or Co. Tyrone. Several saints and four popes have been called Eugene.

Evan

Evan is the Anglicised spelling of Ieuan, or the Welsh form of John, meaning 'Jehovah has been gracious'. The name is popular in Ireland as well as in Wales [see John].

Ferdia

Ferdia means 'man of smoke'. Ferdia was the friend and blood-brother of the great hero Cúchulainn. The story of how Queen Medb tricked Ferdia into fighting a three-day duel with Cúchulainn, who killed him, is told in the Táin Bó Cúailnge, The Cattle Raid of Cooley.

Fergal, Feargal, Fearghal

Fergal means 'brave'. Fergal Mac Maile Dúin of Aileach (d 722) was High King of Ireland. A grisly legend tells how he was defeated in battle by men from Leinster, and his head was stuck on a pike along with the head of Donn Bó, a young musician. Badb, the battle goddess, hovered over them in the shape of a raven, and Donn Bó's head began to sing Fergal's praises. St Fergal – Latinised to Virgil – (d 784) was an Irish scholar, a missionary and bishop of Salzburg. Salzburg Cathedral is dedicated to him.

Fergus, Feargus, Fearghus

Fergus means 'man's strength' or 'man of vigour'. This name was enormously popular in early Irish myth, legend and history. Kings, warriors, poets and saints have all been called Fergus. Fergus Mac Eirc – Fergus Mór the Great – was an Irishman who founded the Scottish kingdom of Dal Riada. Fergus Mac Róich was tricked out of the throne of Ulster by Nessa, mother of Conchobar. As a result, Fergus supported Queen Medb, and fought against Ulster. Centuries later, bards raised Fergus's spirit from his grave and he related the story now known as the Táin Bó Cúailnge.

Fiachra

Some scholars think Fiachra means 'hunt king' or 'battle king'. Others think it means 'raven'. One of the children of Lir, turned into swans by their step-mother in the ancient Irish story, is named Fiachra. St Fiachra (d 670) was an Irish hermit who lived in France. He built a hostel for travellers, and is the patron saint of gardeners. He also gave his name to the fiacre, a Parisien horse-drawn cab.

Finbar, Finbarr
Fionnbharra

Finbar means 'fair-haired'. In folk tales, Fionnbharra was the king of the Connacht fairies, and lord of the dead. At least three saints have been called Finbar. St Finbarr (d around 633) was an abbot and bishop who founded the monastery of Cork, though he probably came from Connacht. In one story, he crossed the Irish Sea on horseback! Finbar Furey is an Irish singer, songwriter and uilleann piper, well known all around the world.

Fintan
Fiontan, Fionntán

Fintan means 'white fire'. According to a very old story, Fintan Mac Bochra was the only Irishman to survive the biblical flood, living for 5,500 years afterwards. At least 74 saints (many are probably imaginary) were called Fintan. St Fintan of Clonenagh (d 603) led a very austere life at the monastery he founded, eating only stale bread and drinking only muddy water.

Fionn
Finn

Fionn means 'white' or 'fair'. Fionn Mac Cumhaill was one of the greatest heroes of Irish legend. Chief of the clan Baiscne, he was also the chief of the Fianna of Erin. He was a bard, a hunter and a great warrior. Fionn was also wise and had the gift of prophecy, having eaten the magical Salmon of Knowledge when he was a boy.

Flann

Flann means 'red' or 'red-haired'. Flann Mac Lonáin was an Irish poet in the 9th and 10th centuries. His satires were so biting that he was nicknamed 'the Devil's Son'. He is supposed to have composed a poem for Angus Óg, the god of love. Flann O'Brien was the pen name of the writer and journalist Brian O'Nolan (1911–66).

Francis
Proinnsias, Proinséas

Francis means either 'free man' or 'Frenchman'. St Francis of Assisi (1181–1226) rejected wealth and chose to live in poverty, helping the sick and the poor. His followers, known as friars, wandered about, teaching, preaching and caring for people. Francis's real name was Giovanni – he was given the nickname Francis because his father had business connections with France. Francis Wheatley (1747–1801) was a painter who eloped to Dublin and painted many Irish subjects. Francis Bacon (1909–92) was a self-taught painter, born in Dublin.

Frank

Frank means 'free' or 'Frenchman'. The Franks were a tribe who migrated from Germany into Gaul in the 4th century, eventually giving their name to the country, France. Today Frank is often used as a short form of Francis or Franklin. Frank O'Connor was the pen name of Michael O'Donovan (1903–66), a writer and playwright and director of the Abbey Theatre who was imprisoned briefly for involvement with the IRA. Frank (Francis) McCourt (1930–2009) was an Irish-American writer who won the Pulitzer Prize in 1997 for *Angela's Ashes*, his account of growing up in Limerick.

Gabriel

 Gabriel is Hebrew and means 'man of God'. In the Bible, Gabriel is one of the archangels. He appears to Daniel in the Old Testament and to Zacharias in the New Testament. Most importantly, he is the Archangel of the Annunciation, appearing to Mary to tell her of the birth of Jesus. Church bells were often dedicated to Gabriel – the Angelus is rung on the Gabriel bell.

Gareth

The origin and meaning of the name Gareth is not clear. Sir Thomas Malory used it in his poem 'Morte d'Arthur' and might have got it from the French Gahariet, though this may be a misreading of a Welsh name. At one point scholars thought it could be connected with the Welsh 'gwared', meaning 'mild' or 'gentle'. Gareth was the younger brother of Sir Gawain and one of King Arthur's Knights of the Round Table. Tennyson also used the name as the hero of his poem 'Gareth and Lynnette'.

Garrett
Gearóid

Garrett is a version of Gerald [see Gerald]. Garrett FitzGerald (1926–2011) was leader of the Fine Gael party and Taoiseach (1982–7).

Gary

Gary is Germanic and means 'spear' or 'spearman'. It can be a shortened form of Gareth [see Gareth] and Garfield, meaning 'battlefield'. Gary Cooper was the stage name of the film star Frank J Cooper (1901–61).

Gavin, Gavan
Garbhan

Gavin comes from the Welsh 'gwalchmai', 'hawk of May' or 'white hawk of May'. Gavin is a version of Gawain, the name of one of the greatest heroes of the Round Table in the stories of King Arthur. Sir Gawain was the son of King Lot of Orkney and Lothian and King Arthur's nephew.

Gearald
Gearalt, Gearóid

Gearóid Og, 11th Earl of Kildare, is supposed to be buried in the rath at Mullaghmast, Co. Kildare. Once every seven years he comes out and rides round the Curragh on a horse with silver shoes. Gearald is a version of Gerald [see Gerald].

George
Seoirse

George is Greek and means 'farmer' or 'tiller of the soil'. St George is the patron saint of England, Germany, Greece and Portugal among others. George Francis FitzGerald (1851–1901) was a physicist and professor of natural philosophy at Dublin. The 'FitzGerald contraction' is an essential part of relativity theory. George Moore (1852–1933) was a writer who pioneered the naturalistic, realistic novel, and helped WB Yeats in planning the Irish National Theatre. George Hook is a popular rugby commentator and broadcaster.

Gerald, Garrett
Gearalt, Gearóid

Gerald is old German and means 'spear rule'. St Gerald (d 732) was one of the English monks who went with St Colman from Lindisfarne to set up a monastery at Inishbofin off the coast of Connacht. Gerald, third Earl of Desmond (1338–98) was supposed to have had a fairy mother and to have been a magician.

Gerard, Gerrard, Garrett

Gerard is old German and means 'brave spear' or 'strong spear'. There are several saints named Gerard. Gerardus Mercator (1512–94) was a Flemish mathematician, geographer and map maker. In 1596 he devised a map projection, named after him, which is still used by navigators. He was the first person to use the word 'atlas' for a book of maps. Gerard 'Gerry' Adams (1948–), Gearóid Mac Ádhaimh, is the president of Sinn Féin and a leading political figure in Northern Ireland.

Gobnait

St Gobnait was born in Co. Clare in the 5th or 6th century and was the patron saint of beekeepers and honeybees. Deborah is the Anglicised form and means 'honeybee'.

Gordon

Gordon means 'hill fort' or 'three-cornered hill'. Gordon was originally a place name in Scotland. Its use as a first name probably comes from the famous British general Charles George Gordon (1833–85), who fought in the Crimean War, put down the Taiping Rebellion in China and, after a ten-month siege, was killed at Khartoum in the Sudan, two days before help arrived.

Gregory

Gregory comes from a Greek word meaning 'watchful'. At least ten saints and 16 popes have been called Gregory. St Gregory the Great (d 604) was the first pope of this name. He founded monasteries, reformed the Church, ransomed prisoners and helped those suffering as a result of war, famine and disease.

Henry, Harry
Anraí, Annraoi, Anraoi

Henry comes from a Frankish word and means 'home-ruler'. Henry the
Navigator (1394–1460) was a Portuguese prince who set up an observatory
and a school of scientific navigation. Henry Grattan (1746–1820) was an
Irish politician and orator. He obtained the right for the Irish parliament to
legislate independently and in 1793 won the right for Catholics to vote.

Hugh

Hugh comes from a Frankish word and means 'heart', 'mind' or
'spirit'. Hugh O'Neill, second Earl of Tyrone (1540–1616) was the last O'Neill
to rule independently. He wanted to rule all Ulster and led a rebellion
against the English, whom he beat at Yellow Ford on the river Blackwater.
He was later defeated, eventually going into exile and dying in Rome. The
name has a long history, appearing in the Domesday Book. Hugh Lane
(1875–1915) established Dublin's Municipal Art Gallery in 1908, now known
as the Hugh Lane Gallery.

Ian, Iain

Ian is the Scottish form of John [see John]. Ian Dempsey is one of Ireland's best known broadcasters. Currently working for Today FM, his big break came when he presented *Dempsey's Den* with puppets Zig and Zag.

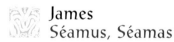 Jack

A pet name for John, but now used in its own right [see John]. It has appeared consistently on top-ten lists for several years, at times taking the number one spot.

Jacob

Jacob is Hebrew and means 'supplanter'. Jacob was one of the patriarchs of the Old Testament. He was the son of Isaac and Rebecca and Esau's younger twin brother. Jacob tricked Esau out of his inheritance and out of his father's blessing. Later, Jacob's 12 sons gave their names to the 12 tribes of Israel.

James
Séamus, Séamas

James is a version of Jacob [see Jacob]. In the New Testament, James is the name of one of Jesus' brothers. James Connolly (1868–1916) was a Scottish socialist and union leader who founded the Irish Socialist Republican Party, *The Workers' Republic* newspaper and the Irish Transport and General Workers' Union. He was one of the executed leaders of he 1916 Rising. James Joyce (1882–1941) was an Irish writer whose revolutionary work changed the way novels were written. James has been a popular name in Ireland for many years.

Jarlath
Iarlaith

Jarlath means 'knight'. One early St Jarlath was converted by St Patrick, and became the third bishop of Armagh. Another St Jarlath (d around 550) was an abbot and bishop who founded a monastery at Cluain Fois near Tuam, as well as founding the diocese of Tuam. Pilgrims used to visit the saint's holy well until the practice was stopped in the 1840s.

Jason

Jason is Greek and means 'healer'. In Greek myth, Jason was a hero who led the Argonauts, a band of warriors who sailed to Colchis to find the Golden Fleece. In the Bible, St Paul stays with a relative called Jason (who was later persecuted) when he visited Thessalonica.

Jeremy

Jeremy is derived from Hebrew and means 'may Jehovah raise up', or 'may Jehovah exalt'. Jeremy is the English form of the name Jeremiah. Jeremiah (around 650–570 BC) was an Old Testament prophet. Jeremy Bentham (1748–1832) was a philosopher and social reformer, who proposed that the proper purpose of government was 'the greatest happiness of the greatest number'.

Jerome

Jerome comes from a Greek word that means 'holy name'. St Jerome (d 420) was a very great biblical scholar. Living in Bethlehem, he translated almost the entire Bible from Hebrew and Greek into Latin. This version, the Vulgate, is still used. St Jerome is often portrayed with a lion sitting beside him.

John
Seán

John is Hebrew and means 'Jehovah has been gracious'. John has been the most popular of all male Christian names. There are 64 saints called John in the Roman calendar alone, including St John the Baptist and St John the Evangelist, who wrote the fourth gospel. Twenty-three popes have used it (25, counting the two popes called John Paul), eight emperors of Byzantium, and kings of European countries including Hungary, Poland, Portugal and France. John Millington Synge (1871–1909) was an outstanding and influential Irish playwright. John McCormack (1884–1945) was a world-famous Irish tenor.

Jonathan

In the Bible, Jonathan is the son of King Saul and the good friend of David. Jonathan Swift (1667–1745) was a clergyman and the most feared political satirist of his time. He was Dean of St Patrick's Cathedral, in Dublin. Many of his tracts and essays support Irish causes, but his best-known work is *Gulliver's Travels*. Jonathan Rhys Meyers is an Irish actor who has found success in Hollywood.

Joseph
Seosamh

Joseph is Hebrew, and means 'God shall add'. In the Old Testament, Joseph was Jacob's favourite son. When he was given a many-coloured coat, his jealous brothers sold him into slavery in Egypt. He became the pharaoh's chief steward, helping his family during a seven-year famine. In the New Testament, St Joseph was the husband of the Virgin Mary. Joseph of Arimathea buried Jesus in his own rock tomb. Limerick-born Joseph O'Mara (1866–1927) was a singer and impresario.

Joshua

Joshua is Hebrew and it means 'Jehovah is salvation'. In the Bible, Joshua was the leader of the Israelites after Moses died. He led the people to the promised land, winning many battles as the Israelites spread out through the country.

Keith

Keith means 'wood'. Keith was originally the name of a place in East Lothian, Scotland. It then became a surname and it was the surname of the hereditary Earls Marshal of Scotland from 1455 to 1715. Finally, it was used as a first name, with a fall in popularity towards the end of the 20th century.

Kenneth

Kenneth means 'handsome'. St Kenneth (d about 600) was an Irish monk who worked in western Scotland, possibly with St Columba. The islet of Inch Kenneth in Mull is named after him. In Ireland, he founded the monastery at Aghaboe in Ossory.

Kevin
Caoimhín

Kevin means 'born beautiful'. St Kevin (d 618) was at first a hermit. Then he moved to Glendalough in Co. Wicklow, where he founded a monastery, though Kevin himself lived in a cave. He loved animals. One story tells of a blackbird that laid an egg in his outstretched hand – St Kevin held it still until the egg had hatched.

Laurence, Lawrence
Labhrás

Laurence comes from the Latin place name Laurentium and means 'of Laurentium' or 'from the place of laurels'. St Laurence (d 258) was a martyred deacon in Rome. St Laurence O'Toole was a 12th-century archbishop of Dublin [see Lorcan].

Lee

Lee is old English and means 'field' or 'meadow'. Lee was originally a place name, which was then used as a surname. It became a popular first name in the USA in honour of the confederate general Robert E Lee (1807–70).

Lewis, Louis

Lewis is Germanic and means 'famous warrior'. Eighteen kings of France have been called Louis. St Louis was Louis IX (1214–70). He reformed the law, wanting justice for all men, and encouraged art and literature.

Liam

Liam is a short form of William, used for that name in Ireland and among people of Irish descent [see William]. Liam Cosgrave (1920–2017) was an Irish politician who served as Taoiseach (1973-7).

Lochlan, Lochlainn

Lochlan originally meant 'lakeland' or 'land of waters', but came to mean 'Viking', 'marauder' or 'robber'. In ancient Irish legend, Lochlainn was the land of dangerous invaders. When Vikings started to raid Ireland in the 8th century, the name was transferred to them, as Irish people thought they could not be beaten. Many chiefs of the clan MacLean in Scotland have been called Lochlan. The name has been Anglicised as Loughlin and Loughlan, with Lachlan as a Scottish variant.

Lorcán

Lorcán means 'fierce'. St Lawrence O'Toole (d 1180) is the English version of the name Lorcán Ua Tuathail. Lorcán was the son of a Leinster chieftain. He became abbot of Glendalough, then archbishop of Dublin.

Luke

Luke comes from the Latin version of a Greek word meaning 'man from Lucania'. St Luke was the third evangelist, generally thought to have written the third gospel and the Acts of the Apostles. Luke is the patron saint of doctors and surgeons, and also of painters, as it was said he painted a picture of the Virgin Mary. The name has become very popular in recent years.

Malachy, Malachi

Malachi means 'my messenger'. Malachi was the last of the 12 minor prophets whose books appear in the Old Testament. St Malachy (1094–1148) was really called Mael Maedoc Ua Morgair. He was bishop of Bangor and Connor, then archbishop of Armagh, doing much to reform the Church and make better links between Ireland and Rome.

Malcolm

Malcolm is Scottish Gaelic and means 'servant of Columba'. Malcolm III of Scotland (around 1031–93) was nicknamed Canmore, or 'big head'. Malcolm's father had been killed by Macbeth, so Malcolm had to defeat and kill Macbeth to take his kingdom.

Manus
Maghnus

Manus is Latin and means 'great'. It is the Irish form of the name Magnus. Seven kings of Norway were called Magnus, as were several Scandinavian saints. St Magnus of Orkney (d around 1116) was the son of Erling, who ruled the Orkney islands. He was noted for his virtue and piety. When King Magnus Barefoot of Norway invaded the islands, Magnus took refuge with King Malcolm Canmore of Scotland.

Mark

Mark comes from the popular Latin name 'Marcus', which is probably connected to Mars, the god of war. In the Bible, St Mark was the author of the second gospel. St Mark's cathedral in Venice was dedicated in 829. Marco Polo (1254–1324) was a Venetian merchant who travelled to China, working for Emperor Kublai Khan for nearly 20 years. Later, he wrote an account of his travels, which became a medieval bestseller.

Martin
Máirtín

Martin is Latin and means 'of Mars', or 'warlike'. St Martin (d 397) was a Roman soldier who cut his cloak in half so he could clothe a beggar. Afterwards, he was baptised, eventually becoming bishop of Tours in France. He was an active missionary and set up many monasteries.

Matthew
Maitiú

Matthew is Hebrew and means 'gift of Jehovah'. In the Bible, St Matthew was a tax collector whom Jesus called to be a disciple. Later, he wrote the first gospel. He is the patron saint of accountants, bankers, bookkeepers and tax collectors. St Matthias was chosen as an apostle to replace Judas Iscariot. His name is the Greek form of Matthew, spelled this way so the two saints are not confused.

Maurice
Muiris

Maurice comes from a Latin word meaning 'Moorish' or 'dark-skinned'. Muiris Ó Súilleabháin (1904–50) was the author of *Fiche Bliain ag Fás*, or *Twenty Years A-Growing*, a memoir of growing up on Great Blasket Island.

Michael
Mícheál

Michael is Hebrew and means 'who is like God'. Michael is one of the archangels, honoured by Christians, Jews and Muslims. In the Book of Revelation, Michael led the heavenly host when there was war in heaven, defeating the forces of Lucifer. He is the patron saint of Germany, and of grocers, paratroopers, policemen, radiologists and sick people. Michael Collins (1890–1922) was an Irish nationalist and politician who negotiated the treaty with Britain in 1921. Mícheál Mac Liammóir (1899–1978) was an Irish actor and playwright.

Miles, Myles, Milo

Some scholars think Miles may be from the Latin word 'miles', meaning 'soldier'. Others think it could be connected to the old Slavonic 'milu', meaning 'merciful'. In Ireland, the name Maol Mhuire, meaning 'servant of Mary', is used by men and women. Men have used Miles as an Anglicised version of the name. Myles na Gopaleen was a pen name of Brian O'Nolan (1911–66), the novelist and journalist also known as Flann O'Brien.

Murrough

Murrough means 'sea warrior'. Murrough O'Brien, first Earl of Inchiquin (1618–74) was heavily involved in the fighting that took place in Ireland during the English Civil War.

Murtagh

Murtagh is the Irish version of Murdoch or Murdo. Murtagh means 'skilled in seacraft' or 'sea lord'. Muircheartach Mac Erca was a legendary high king about whom many stories were told. He was supposed to have sent the Lia Fáil, the stone on which Irish kings were crowned, to his brother Fergus Mac Eirc in Scotland for his coronation. Fergus reputedly refused to give it back. Muircheartach Ua Briain (Murtough O'Brien) was high king of Ireland (1086–1114), the last O'Brien and the second-to-last high king.

Naoise

In mythology, Naoise was the lover of Deirdre who was imprisoned in the tower by Conchobar Mac Nessa.

Nathan

In the Bible, Nathan was the prophet who was brave enough to tell King David he had done wrong after David had put Uriah the Hittite into the front line of battle so he would be killed. David called one of his own sons Nathan. It is sometimes used as a short form of Nathaniel and of Jonathan. Nathan is Hebrew and means 'gift'.

Niall
Neil

Niall of the Nine Hostages, or Niall Noígíallach (d 405), was the first historical high king of Ireland. Some scholars think Niall's nickname may refer to hostages taken from the Airgialla, small kingdoms in the north of Ireland that he conquered. Another theory is that he took one hostage from each of the five kingdoms of Ireland, and one each from the Scots, the Saxons, the British and the French. The Uí Néill dynasty is descended from him. Niall may come from nel, meaning 'a cloud' or from niadh or niul, meaning 'champion'.

Nicholas
Nioclás

Nicholas is Greek and means 'victory of the people'. St Nicholas was the 4th-century bishop of Myra in Asia Minor. There are many stories about him, including one in which he helped three poor girls by throwing bags of gold for their dowries through their window at night. St Nicholas is the patron saint of Russia and of Greece. He is also the patron saint of brewers, fishermen, merchants, pawnbrokers and children, to whom he gives presents at Christmas. He is the origin of Father Christmas, and Santa Claus comes from Sinter Klaas, the Dutch version of his name.

Odhran, Odran, Oran

Odhran means 'dun' or 'sallow'. More than 20 saints have been
called Odhran – one was St Patrick's charioteer. On a journey to Munster,
Odhran suspected that an attempt would be made to ambush and kill
Patrick. Odhran said he felt ill, and persuaded the saint to drive the chariot.
They changed places and when eventually they were ambushed, it was
Odhran who was killed with the spear intended for Patrick.

Oengus, Aonghus
Angus

Oengus is the old Irish spelling of Angus [see Angus]. In Irish myth,
Oenghus was the son of the Dagda, the chief god of ancient Ireland. His
mother was Bóinn, goddess of the river now called the Boyne. Oengus Óg
was the god of youth, beauty and love.

Oisín
Ossian

Oisín means 'little deer'. Oisín was the son of Fionn Mac Cumhaill. His mother was magically turned into a doe, and he was raised in the wild for seven years. Oisín, one of the greatest warriors of the Fianna, was lured away to Tír na nÓg by Niamh. He thought he had spent just one day in the Land of Youth, but he had been there, unchanged by time, for 300 years. When Oisín wanted to go back to Ireland, Niamh told him not to get off his fairy horse, but he leaned down to help some men move a stone and the harness broke. Oisín fell to the ground, and instantly aged 300 years, dying soon after. Oisín is currently in vogue as a name for boys.

Oscar, Osgur

Oscar means 'deer lover'. Oscar was the son of Oisín and the grandson of Fionn Mac Cumhaill. He was the best of the Fianna, the bravest, the strongest and the most victorious. He was also a poet. Oscar died in battle with one of the Fianna's great enemies, Cairbre Lifechair, who put a spear through the hero at the same moment Oscar killed him. The only time Fionn was ever seen to weep was at Oscar's death. Oscar Wilde (1854–1900) was an Irish playwright, poet and storyteller. Oscar frequently makes an appearance in the top 100 names for boys in Ireland.

Owen
Eoin

Owen is the Welsh version of the Latin name Eugenius, meaning 'well-born'. Owain Glyndyfrdwy, or Owen Glendower (d 1416) was a Welsh chief, educated in England. In 1401 he proclaimed himself Prince of Wales and set up a Welsh parliament. He joined English nobles rebelling against the king, Henry IV, but was defeated at Shrewsbury. Owen Glendower continued to fight for Welsh independence until he died.

 ## Patrick
Pádraig, Pádraic

Patrick comes from the Latin Patricius and means 'a patrician' or 'of noble birth'. St Patrick (around 385–461) was originally called Sucat, but chose the name Patrick when he became a missionary. Patrick first went to Ireland as a slave. After six years he escaped, trained as a priest in France, then returned to Ireland as a missionary bishop. Patrick Sarsfield (d 1693) defeated the English at Sligo. He defended Limerick and, when it surrendered, he was allowed to leave Ireland with an Irish army (the Flight of the Wild Geese), taking service in France. Pádraic Pearse was a writer and nationalist, and was commander-in-chief of the insurgents during the Easter Rising of 1916. It has been one of the most popular names for Irish boys for many years.

 ## Paul
Pól

Paul is Latin and means 'little'. St Paul (d around AD 69) was a Pharisee, a strictly observant Jew, and also a Roman citizen. At first Paul persecuted Christians, then, on a visit to Damascus, he was converted after a blinding revelation. Belfast-born Paul Henry (1876–1958) was an influential artist who spent ten years living and painting on Achill Island. Later he was one of the founders of the Society of Dublin Painters.

 ## Peter
Peadar

Jesus gave Simon the fisherman the Aramaic name Kephas, translated in Latin as Petrus, meaning 'stone' or 'rock'. St Peter (d around AD 64) was a fisherman named Simon on the Sea of Galilee when he was called to be a disciple. After the Resurrection, Peter was the leader of the apostles. Traditionally, Peter was the first pope and was martyred in Rome.

 ## Philip
Pilib

Philip is Greek and means 'lover of horses'. There have been several saints called Philip. The first St Philip was one of the 12 disciples. St Philip Neri (1515–95) worked among the young men of Rome and founded a group of laymen who helped pilgrims and looked after the sick – this turned into the Trinity Hospital.

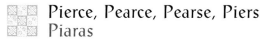 ## Pierce, Pearce, Pearse, Piers
Piaras

Pierce is a surname form of Piers, now used as a first name. Piers is a version of Peter [see Peter]. Sir Piaras Feiritéir of Corkaguiny (d 1653) was one of a group of Irish noblemen who wrote courtly love poems. Piaras Béaslai (1881–1965) was a writer and journalist who fought in the 1916 Rising and the War of Independence.

 ## Proinnsias, Proinséas
Francis

Proinnsias is the Gaelic version of Francis [see Francis].

Rowan Ross
Raymond Redmond
Ryan Ross
Ryan Raymond
Rory Ronan
Richard Ronan
Robert

 ## Raymond, Redmond
Réamonn

Raymond is Germanic and means 'wise protector'. Redmond is a popular name in Northern Ireland, thanks to the tales of the rapparee Count Redmond O'Hanlon (around 1640–1681), portrayed in urban legend as a real-life Robin Hood.

 ## Richard
Risteárd

Richard comes from two Frankish words meaning 'brave king' or 'powerful king'. Richard de Clare, Earl of Pembroke (around 1130–76), known as Strongbow, provoked the English invasion of Ireland in 1171 by marrying Diarmait Mac Murchada's daughter and succeeding to the kingdom of Leinster. Richard 'Mad Dick' Talbot, Earl of Tyrconnell (1630–91), was a Catholic supporter of the Stuarts, satirised in the song 'Lillibullero'. He fought for the Irish Confederacy, survived the Siege of Drogheda and was appointed as head of the Irish Army and lord deputy.

 Robert
Róibéard

Robert comes from two old German words and means 'bright fame'. Robert Boyle (1627–91) was an Irishman often called 'the father of modern chemistry'. He defined elements, and is famous for proposing Boyle's Law, which deals with the pressure and volume of gas. Robert Emmet (1778–1803) was a Protestant revolutionary who joined the United Irishmen and tried to raise a rebellion. This failed and he was betrayed, condemned and executed.

Rónán
Ronan

Rónán means 'little seal'. At least ten saints and several kings have been called Rónán. Rónán (d 624) was a king of Munster who listened to a false accusation against his son and then killed him. St Rónán the Silent went to live as a hermit in Brittany, where the town of Locronan commemorates him. He converted many to Christianity because of his charity and patience. St Rónán had a pet wolf.

Rory
Ruairí, Ruaidhrí

Rory means 'red', 'red-haired' or 'fiery'. Ruaidhrí Ua Conchobar – Rory O'Connor (1166–86) – was the last high king of Ireland.

Ross

Ross means 'promontory' or 'headland', and was originally a place name. It was then used as a surname and later as a first name. There is a large clan Ross, whose home territory was originally Ross and Cromarty in north-east Scotland. Members of the clan have been active in Scottish history since 1214, when the chief and his men helped King Alexander II put down a rebellion.

Rowan
Ruán, Ruadhán

Rowan means 'little red one'. In the ancient tales and legends of Ireland, the rowan tree or mountain ash – sorbus aucuparia – was highly magical. The Salmon of Knowledge ate the rowan berries that fell into the pool where he lived. Stories about St Ruadhán (d 584) are also often magical. He was said to have founded the monastery at Lorrha, where there was a wonderful tree whose sap gave food and drink to anyone who tasted it.

Ryan
Riain

Ryan was originally a surname, now sometimes used as a first name. It means 'chief' or 'king'.

Samuel

Samuel is Hebrew and probably means 'God has heard'. In the Bible, Samuel (11th century BC) was historically extremely important as the last judge and first prophet of Israel. Samuel Beckett (1906–89) was an Irish writer, playright and poet who was awarded the Nobel Prize for Literature in 1969.

Saoirse

Saoirse means 'freedom'. It is a modern name, first used in the 20th century and celebrates Ireland becoming independent.

Scott

Scott was originally a surname, describing someone who came from Scotland. The Scotts were also one of the clans who raided from Scotland over the border into England. F Scott Fitzgerald (1896–1940) was an American novelist who captured the spirit of the Jazz Age in books such as *The Great Gatsby*.

Séamas, Seamus
James

Seamus Heaney (1939–2013) was an Irish poet who won the Nobel Prize for Literature in 1995. Seamus is the Irish version of James, which itself is a version of Jacob [see James and Jacob].

Seán
John, Shaun, Shawn

Seán is the Irish version of John [see John]. Seán Lemass (1899–1971) was Taoiseach (1959–66). Jack Lynch – Seán Ó Loinsigh (1917–99) – was also Taoiseach (1966–73 and 1977–9). Seán O'Casey (1884–1964) was a playwright whose anti-war work, *The Plough and the Stars*, caused a riot. Seán Ó Riada (1931–71) was an outstanding and influential composer whose work ranged from the avant garde through work for theatre and films to achieving a revival of interest in traditional Irish music, especially through his band Ceoltóiri Chualann.

Seosamh
Joseph

Seosamh is the Gaelic form of Joseph [see Joseph]. Seosamh Ó hÉanaí (1919–84) was an Irish folk singer from Carna, Connemara, who moved to the USA to sing and teach.

Setanta

Setanta relates to a Celtic tribe, the Setantii, which settled in Britain. Setanta was the first name of the great Irish hero Cúchulainn, who was only seven when he changed his name. Conchobar Mac Nessa, king of Ulster, was the boy's foster-father. He and his court had been invited to dine with Culann, a rich smith. Setanta arrived late and had to kill Culann's ferocious guard dog to gain entry. Culann was upset at the loss of his dog, so Setanta said he would be Culann's hound while another guard dog was trained. 'Cú' means 'hound' and 'Chulainn' means 'of Culann' or 'of the smith'. A modern-day Setanta is the Cork hurler Setanta Ó hAilpín.

Shane

Shane is an Anglicised version of Seán found in Northern Ireland [see Seán, John].

Simon
Síomón

Simon is Hebrew and means 'hearkening' or 'hearing with acceptance'. There are eight men called Simon in the New Testament and others in both the Old and New Testaments called Simeon, another spelling of the same name. St Peter's name was Simon before Jesus called him as a disciple and named him Peter. St Simon the Zealot was another disciple: he may have taught in Egypt and Persia and been martyred in Persia.

Stephen, Steven
Stiofán, Steafán

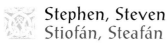

St Stephen (d around AD 35) was the first Christian martyr. He was also a preacher, and was denounced for blasphemy.

Stewart

Stewart was originally a surname, later used as a first name. It was found i especially n Scotland, where the Stewarts (later spelled in the French way, Stuart) became the royal house. Stewart described a person's occupation. It is old English and means 'steward' or 'housekeeper'. Charles Stewart Parnell (1846–91) was an influential and popular politician who was president of the Land League. He forced major changes to the 1881 Land Act and pressured Gladstone to introduce the Irish Home Rule Bill of 1886. Parnell's career finished when his association with Kitty O'Shea resulted in his being cited as co-respondent in the O'Sheas' divorce.

Tadg, Tadhg

Tadg was originally a nickname, meaning 'poet' or 'philosopher'. Tadg Mac Céin was a legendary hero who had a vision of the beautiful goddess Clíodhna, with three lovely birds. Tadg also had adventures in the Underworld. In one he came to an island where, according to a woman he met, all the kings of Ireland after Conn of the Hundred Battles had lived. When Tadg returned to Ireland, he found that a whole year had gone by. Tadg was such a popular name that it was used in several phrases, such as Tadhg na Sráide – meaning 'Tadg in the street' or 'man in the street'.

Terence

Terence comes from Terentius, the name of a Roman clan or family. Terence MacSwiney (1879–1920) was an Irish Nationalist who took part in the Easter Rising. Later he became lord mayor of Cork. Arrested on a charge of sedition, he went on hunger strike and died after 74 days. It was the longest hunger strike in Irish political history. Terence O'Neill (1914–90) was a prime minister of Northern Ireland who tried to promote cross-border links with the Republic.

Thomas
Tomás

Thomas is Aramaic and means 'twin'. St Thomas was one of the 12 disciples called by Jesus. He is known as 'doubting Thomas', because he would not accept the Resurrection unless he could see Jesus himself and touch his wounds. Thomas Moore (1779–1852) was a poet and musician whose Irish melodies included songs such as 'The Last Rose of Summer', 'The Minstrel Boy' and 'The Harp that Once Through Tara's Halls'. Thomas McDonagh (1878–1916) was one of the signatories to the Proclamation of Independence. He was executed after the Easter Rising.

Tiernan
Tiarnán, Tighearnán

Ua Tighearnáin is an Irish surname, now also used as a first name. Tiernan is a pet form of tighearna, or tiarna, which means 'lord'. Tighearnach (d 1088) was the abbot of Clonmacnoise. He is reputed to be the author of the *Annals of Tighernach*, the oldest known Irish historical record.

Timothy

Timothy is Greek and means 'honouring God'. St Timothy was converted by St Paul, and became his companion and helper. Later, he was put in charge of the church at Ephesus, and St Paul wrote him two letters which now appear in the New Testament.

Trevor

Trevor was originally the name of a place and was then used as a surname. Later it became a popular first name. Trevor comes from Welsh or Cornish, and means 'big settlement'.

Turlough

Turlough was originally a nickname, meaning 'the instigator'. Two of the last High Kings of Ireland were called Turlough – Tairrdelbach Ua Briain (1072–86) and Tairrdelbach Ua Conchobair (1118–56). Turlough O'Carolan (1670–1738) was an Irish harpist. When he was 18 he caught smallpox and went blind, but this did not stop him from becoming one of Ireland's most famous musicians and composers – over 200 of his pieces survive him.

Vincent
Uinseann, Uinsionn

Vincent is Latin in origin and means 'conquering'. There are several saints called Vincent. St Vincent de Paul (around 1580–1660) was a French priest who was captured by pirates and sold into slavery. He escaped, worked among peasants and convicts, then decided to spend his life serving the poor. He founded the Lazarists, a society of missionary priests, and the Little Sisters of the Poor, an order for women.

William
Uilliam

William comes from two German words meaning 'resolute helmet'. William Butler Yeats (1865–1939) was an Irish poet and playwright. He was influenced by his studies of Irish folklore, and was awarded the Nobel Prize for Literature in 1923. William Conor (1881–1968) was a war artist, portrait painter and muralist who is particularly esteemed for his paintings of Ulster working-class people.

Irish Names for Children Pronunciation guide

GIRLS	PRONUNCIATION
Aibigéal	*ah-be-gale*
Aifric	*aff-rick*
Ailbhe	*al-va*
Ailis, Ailís	*ale-ish, ale-eesh*
Áine	*awn-ya*
Aingeal	*ang-el*
Aisling, Aislinn	*ashling*
Alanna, Alannah	*a-lann-a*
Allsún	*ol-soon*
Aoibheann, Aoibhinn	*ee-van, aye-veen*
Aoife	*ee-fa*
Báirbre	*bar-bra*
Bébhinn	*bay-vin*
Bláthnaid, Báthnait	*blon-id, blon-it*
Brianna	*bree-anna*
Bríghid, Bríd	*breed*
Brónach	*broh-na*
Cailín	*colleen*
Caireann	*kar-en*
Caitlín	*cat-leen*
Caitrín	*cat-reen*
Caitríona	*cat-ree-on-a*

Caoilfhionn	*keelin*
Caoimhe	*kwee-va*
Cara	*car-a*
Ciara, Kiera	*keer-a*
Clíona, Clíodhna	*klee-on-a*
Clodagh	*klo-da*
Cristín	*christine*
Cristíona	*kris-tee-on-a*
Cuileann	*kwill-an*
Darina, Dáiríne	*da-reen-a, daw-reen-a*
Dearbhaile	*dervla*
Deirbhile	*der-vila*
Deirdre	*deer-dra*
Doireann	*dhirr-un*
Éabha	*aye-va*
Éadaoin	*aid-een*
Eavan	*eh-van*
Eibhlín	*ev-leen*
Eileanóir	*el-a-nore*
Eileanóra	*el-a-nora*
Eilís	*eye-leesh*
Eithne, Ethna	*eth-na*
Emer, Éimear	*ee-mer, ay-mer*
Eimíle	*e-mee-la*
Enya	*en-ya*
Étáin	*ay-tawn*
Etaoin	*eh-tane*

Fidelma	*fid-el-ma*
Fiona, Fíne	*fee-o-na, fee-na*
Fionnuala	*fin-oo-la*
Finola	*fin-o-la*
Grania, Gráinne	*graw-nya*
Íde	*ee-da*
Isibéal	*is-a-bale*
Iseult	*is-ult*
Jacinta	*ja-sin-ta*
Laoise	*leash-a*
Líadain	*lee-a-dun*
Loiseach, Luighseach	*li-shock*
Méabh, Meadhbh, Medb	*maeve*
Máiréad	*mawr-aid*
Muireann	*mwir-ann*
Máire	*maura*
Máirín	*maureen*
Neasa	*nass-a*
Niamh	*nee-av*
Nóra	*nora*
Nóirín	*noreen*
Nuala	*noo-la*
Orlaith, Orlagh	*orla*
Orna	*or-na*
Póilín	*pole-een*
Proinnsias	*prun-she-as*
Próinséas	*prone-shay-as*

Ríoghnach, Ríonach	*ree-o-nakh*
Róise	*roy-sha*
Róisín	*ro-sheen*
Rós	*rose*
Sadbh, Sadhbh	*sive [rhy. with hive]*
Saoirse	*sayr-sha, seer-sha*
Séarlait	*share-let*
Seosaimhín	*show-sa-veen*
Sibéal	*sib-ale*
Síle	*sheila, she-la*
Síne	*she-na*
Sinéad	*shin-aid*
Siobhán	*shiv-awn*
Sionainn	*shun-unn*
Siún	*shoon*
Sorcha	*surra-cah*
Toiréasa	*tur-ay-sa*
Treasa	*trass-a*
Tríona	*tree-on-a*
Ríona	*ree-on-a*
Úna	*oona*

BOYS	PRONUNCIATION
Aedán, Aodhán	*ay-dawn*
Ailin	*al-in*
Aindriú	*an-drew*
Aonghus, Oengus	*ain-gus*
Anraí, Annraoi, Anraoi	*on-ree*
Antóin	*ant-own*
Bairtliméad	*bart-le-made*
Bearach	*bear-ock*
Beartlaoi	*bart-lee*
Breandán	*bran-dawn*
Briain	*bree-an*
Cahal, Cathal	*ka-hull*
Caoimhín	*kwee-veen*
Cian	*key-un*
Ciarán	*keer-awn*
Cóilín	*ko-leen*
Colm, Colum, Columb	*koll-um*
Colmán	*kol-mawn*
Conall	*kon-al*
Conán	*ko-nawn*
Conchobhar	*konner*
Conn	*kon*
Críostóir	*kris-tore*
Dáibhéad	*daw-vade*
Dáibhíd	*daw-veed*
Daire	*dara*

Dáithí	*daw-hee*
Déaglán	*day-glawn*
Diarmaid	*dear-mid*
Diarmait	*dear-mat*
Diarmuid	*dear-mwid*
Deasún	*dass-oon*
Dónal, Domhnall	*dough-null*
Donncha, Donnchadh	*don-a-ka*
Donogh, Donough	*done-a*
Duane	*dwan*
Éamon, Éamonn	*ay-mon*
Éanna	*ay-nah*
Eógan	*owe-gawn*
Eoghan	*owen*
Eoin	*owen, owe-in*
Feargus, Fearghus	*fergus*
Ferdia	*fur-dee-a*
Fergal, Feargal, Fearghal	*fur-gull*
Fiachra	*fee-a-kra*
Fionn	*fyun, fin*
Fionnbharra	*fin-barra*
Fiontan, Fionntán	*fin-tun, fin-tawn*
Garbhan	*gar-vun*
Gearalt	*garr-ult*
Gearóid	*garr-ode*
Iarlaith	*ear-la*
Labhrás	*lao-rawss*

Liam	*lee-am*
Lochlan, Lochlainn	*lock-lan*
Lorcán	*lore-cawn*
Malachy	*mal-a-key*
Maghnus	*manus*
Máirtín	*mar-teen*
Maitiú	*mat-you*
Muiris	*mwir-ish*
Mícheál	*mee-hawl*
Murrough	*mur-ra*
Murtagh	*mur-ta*
Naoise	*nee-sha*
Niall	*nigh-al*
Nioclás	*nick-lawss*
Odhran, Odran, Oran	*or-en*
Oengus, Aonghus	*ain-gus*
Oisín, Ossian	*ush-een*
Pádraig, Pádraic	*paw-drig, paw-drick, paw-ric*
Peadar	*padder*
Piaras	*peer-us*
Pilib	*pill-ub*
Pól	*pole*
Proinnsias	*prun-she-as*
Proinséas	*prun-shay-as*
Réamonn	*ray-mon*
Ríain	*ree-an*
Risteárd	*rish-tard*

Róibéard	*roy-bared*
Rónán	*row-nawn*
Ruairí, Ruaidhrí	*rory*
Ruán, Ruadhán	*rue-awn*
Saoirse	*sayr-sha*
Séamas, Seamus	*shame-us*
Seán	*shaun, shawn*
Seoirse	*ssore-sha*
Seosamh	*show-suv*
Setanta	*sa-tan-ta*
Síomón	*see-mawn*
Stiofán, Steafán	*stiff-awn*
Tadg, Tadhg	*tige [tiger without the 'r']*
Tiernán, Tighernán	*tier-nawn*
Tomás	*tom-awss*
Turlough	*tur-lock*
Uinseann, Uinsionn	*in-shin*
Uilliam	*oo-lyum*

Saint's day guide

JANUARY

1st	*Mary Mother of God*
	Oisín
	Fainche
2nd	*Mainchín*
3rd	*Killian*
4th	*Aodh*
5th	*Ciarán*
6th	*Dermot*
7th	*Donnán*
	Eimhín
8th	*Finán*
9th	*Faolán*
	Brendan
10th	*Dermot*
11th	*Ronan*
	Suibhne
12th	*Conan*
	Cumín
13th	*Colmán*
	Ronan
14th	*Flann*
15th	*Aithche*
16th	*Dermot*
	Maelíosa

17th	*Ernan*
	Ultan
19th	*Fachtna*
	Suibhne
20th	*Aonghus*
	Fergus
	Fechin
21st	*Flann*
	Fainche
22nd	*Lonan*
23rd	*Lucan*
	Canice
25th	*Aodh*
26th	*Ernin*
27th	*Lucan*
28th	*Mellan*
29th	*Cronan*
	Bláth
30th	*Enan*
	Ailbe
31st	*Aidan*
	Canice

FEBRUARY

1st	*Brigid*
2nd	*Colmán*
3rd	*Keelin*
4th	*Ciarán*
	Loman
5th	*Finghin*
6th	*Colm*
7th	*Mellan*
	Aodh
	Loman
	Lonan
8th	*Fiachra*
	Fáilbhe
9th	*Ronan*
	Ríonach
10th	*Cronan*
11th	*Finnian*
	Gobnait
12th	*Aloysius*
	Siadhal
13th	*Conan*
	Finan
14th	*Mainchín*
	Caomhán
15th	*Fergus*
	Bearach
16th	*Aonghus*

16th	*Aodh*
17th	*Cormac*
	Fintan
18th	*Colmán*
	Aonghus
19th	*Odrán*
	Fechin
20th	*Cronan*
21st	*Colmán*
	Fintan
22nd	*Caomhán*
23rd	*Ernin*
24th	*Ciarán*
	Cumín
25th	*Cianán*
26th	*Beacan*
	Eithne
27th	*Comhghan*
28th	*Ernin*

MARCH

1st	*Colm*
	Seanán
2nd	*Cuan*
	Finnian
	Conall
3rd	*Killian*
	Fachtna

5th	*Carthach*
	Ciarán
6th	*Cairbre*
	Odrán
	Brigid
8th	*Conan*
	Cronan
	Siadhal
9th	*Aloysius*
	Proinnséas
	Séadna
	Brigid
10th	*Colmán*
	Fáilbhe
11th	*Aonghus*
12th	*Killian*
13th	*Caomhán*
14th	*Ultan*
	Flannán
15th	*Eoghan*
16th	*Aidan*
	Finan
	Abban
17th	*Patrick*
	Beacan
	Tierney

18th	*Coman*
	Caomhán
	Conall
20th	*Conan*
	Aidan
21st	*Enda*
22nd	*Fáilbhe*
23rd	*Fergus*
	Mainchín
24th	*Aloysius*
25th	*Enan*
26th	*Cormac*
	Carthach
	Garvan
27th	*Fintan*
28th	*Conall*
29th	*Aidan*
	Eithne
30th	*Colman*
	Fergus
31st	*Faolán*

APRIL

1st	*Celsus*
	Aidan
2nd	*Conall*
3rd	*Coman*

4th	*Ultan*	20th	*Flann*
	Tierney		*Enan*
	Colmán		*Donnán*
5th	*Beacan*	21st	*Bearach*
7th	*Finan*	22nd	*Callaghan*
	Seanán	24th	*Dermot*
	Aodh	26th	*Beacon*
8th	*Ronan*		*Cronan*
	Fáilbhe		*Dónal*
	Tiernan		*Conan*
9th	*Colmán*	27th	*Ultan*
10th	*Bercan*	28th	*Cronan*
	Killian		*Suibhne*
11th	*Aodh*	30th	*Ronan*
	Maodhúg		*Ciarán*
12th	*Ernin*		
14th	*Colmán*	**MAY**	
	Killian	1st	*Ultan*
15th	*Ruadhán*		*Ronan*
16th	*Ultan*		*Oisín*
	Fáilbhe		*Mainchín*
17th	*Garvan*	2nd	*Enan*
	Aloysius		*Colmán*
	Eochaidh		*Fiachra*
	Donnán	3rd	*Cairbre*
18th	*Eoghan*		*Conley*
	Laserian	4th	*Aodh*
			Cronan

5th	Seanán		19th	Cumín
	Faolán			Ciarán
6th	Colmán			Richella
7th	Bercan		20th	Colmán
8th	Coman		21st	Cumín
	Odrán			Ronan
	Brendan			Finbar
10th	Cathal			Brigid
	Aodh		22nd	Ronan
	Comhghall			Conall
11th	Kevin			Aloysius
	Fintan			Aghna
12th	Ernin			Luighseach
13th	Tierney		23rd	Criomhthann
14th	Garvan			Coman
	Carthach		24th	Bercan
15th	Coman			Colmán
	Muireadhach			Ultan
	Colm		25th	Donnchadh
	Dymphna		26th	Colmán
16th	Brendan			Beacan
	Odrán		27th	Killian
	Ernan		28th	Eoghan
17th	Finnian			Faolán
18th	Bran		31st	Ernin
	Breasal			Eoghan
	Colmán			
	Aghna			

JUNE

1st	*Cronan*
	Colmán
	Cumín
2nd	*Aidan*
	Seanán
3rd	*Kevin*
4th	*Colm*
	Ernin
	Colmán
5th	*Bercan*
6th	*Jarlath*
	Colmán
	Faolán
	Lonan
7th	*Caomhán*
	Colm
9th	*Colm*
10th	*Bearach*
12th	*Giolla*
	Chríost
	Cronan
	Caomhán
13th	*Kerill*
	Dymphna
14th	*Ciarán*
15th	*Colmán*

16th	*Sáadna*
17th	*Aidan*
	Colmán
18th	*Colmán*
19th	*Fáilbhe*
	Caolán
20th	*Faolán*
21st	*Dermot*
	Suibhne
	Cormac
22nd	*Cronan*
	Suibhne
23rd	*Faolán*
24th	*Cormac*
26th	*Colmán*
27th	*Aodh*
28th	*Ernin*
30th	*Fáilbhe*
	Caolán

JULY

1st	*Cumín*
	Ernin
	Ultan
	Conan
3rd	*Killian*
	Ultan
	Maolmhuire

4th	Finbar		18th	Fintan
5th	Fergus			Cronan
	Ultan			Celsus
	Éadaoin			Fáilbhe
6th	Eithne		19th	Oisín
	Blinne			Colmán
7th	Tierney			Ciarán
	Maelruain			Aidan
8th	Dermot			Fergus
	Killian		20th	Fáilbhe
	Colmán		22nd	Oisín
	Tadhg			Colmán
9th	Garvan		24th	Declan
10th	Ultan			Cronan
	Aodh			Comhghall
	Cuan		25th	Finbar
	Seanán			Fiachra
11th	Fáilbhe			Nessan
	Colmán			Caolán
	Lonan			Colmán
12th	Colmán		27th	Brendan
	Ultan		28th	Comhghall
13th	Fintan		29th	Coman
	Ernin			Cumín
14th	Colmán			Caolán
15th	Ronan		31st	Colmán
	Colmán			
17th	Flann			

AUGUST

1st	Colm
	Fáilbhe
2nd	Lonan
	Fechin
	Comhghan
3rd	Aidan
	Feidhlimidh
	Crohan
4th	Molua
5th	Colman
	Ernin
	Ranait
6th	Aloysius
7th	Cronan
	Killian
	Aidan
	Seanán
8th	Colmán
9th	Ultan
	Ciarán
	Feidhlimidh
10th	Cumín
11th	Donnán
	Athracht
12th	Lucan
	Iomhar
	Brigid

13th	Laserian
	Muireadhach
14th	Fachtna
	Cumín
	Caomhán
15th	Colmán
	Aodh
16th	Conan
17th	Beacan
	Seanán
	Ernan
18th	Ernin
	Colmán
	Odrán
	Ronan
19th	Enan
22nd	Cumín
23rd	Eoghan
24th	Faolán
26th	Comhghall
	Faolán
27th	Aidan
28th	Feidhlimidh
30th	Cronan
	Fiachra
31st	Aidan
	Killian
	Aodh

SEPTEMBER

1st	*Cumín*
	Fáilbhe
2nd	*Colm*
	Enan
	Seanán
3rd	*Colmán*
4th	*Ultan*
	Fiachra
	Comhghall
	Aidan
	Seanán
	Cumín
6th	*Colm*
	Colmán
7th	*Ultan*
8th	*Birth of Mary*
	Fergus
	Fintan
9th	*Ciarán*
	Finbar
	Conall
10th	*Finbar*
	Odrán
	Fergus
	Finnian
11th	*Colmán*
12th	*Ailbe*
	Colmán
13th	*Naomhán*
14th	*Cormac*
	Caomhán
	Ailbhe
15th	*Our Lady of Sorrows*
16th	*Laserian*
	Colmán
	Seanán
17th	*Cumín*
19th	*Fintan*
20th	*Aidan*
22nd	*Aodh*
	Colm
	Colmán
23rd	*Adomnán*
24th	*Callaghan*
25th	*Finbar*
	Colmán
	Seanán
26th	*Colmán*
27th	*Finnian*
28th	*Dermot*
	Fiachra

29th	Colm	11th	Loman	
	Ciarán		Canice	
	Nessan	12th	Dermot	
	Comhghall		Fiachra	
30th	Faolán		Aidan	
	Aloysius		Faolán	
	Brigid	13th	Comhghan	
	Colmán	14th	Colm	
		15th	Cuan	
OCTOBER			Colmán	
1st	Fintan		Cormac	
	Colm	16th	Eoghan	
	Colmán		Colm	
2nd	Odrán		Kevin	
4th	Finan		Caomhán	
	Colmán	18th	Colmán	
	Seanán	19th	Cronan	
5th	Baothghalach		Colmán	
6th	Aloysius		Faolán	
	Aodh	20th	Aidan	
	Colmán		Fintan	
7th	Celsus	21st	Fintan	
	Comhghall		Mainchín	
8th	Ciarán	22nd	Killian	
9th	Aidan	23rd	Killian	
	Fintan	24th	Colmán	
10th	Fintan		Lonan	
	Seanán	25th	Laserian	

26th *Ernan*
      Odrán
27th *Colmán*
      Odrán
      Ernan
28th *Suibhne*
      Conan
      Colmán
29th *Cuan*
      Aodh
      Colmán
      Caolán
30th *Colmán*
      Feidhlimidh
31st *Faolán*
      Comán

NOVEMBER

1st   *All Saints' Day*
      Cairbre
      Lonan
      Brendan
      Cronan
      Aodh
2nd   *Aloysius*
      Aidan
      Caoimhe
3rd   *Caomhán*

4th   *Tierney*
5th   *Colmán*
      Faolán
      Flannán
6th   *All Saints of Ireland*
      Cronan
      Aidan
7th   *Colmán*
      Fintan
8th   *Colm*
9th   *Beineún*
      Fintan
      Aodhnait
10th *Aodh*
      Coman
      Fergus
      Ciarán
11th *Cronan*
      Cairbre
      Dubhán
12th *Cumín*
      Ernin
      Lonan
      Mainchín
13th *Ernin*
      Odharnait
14th *Lorcán*
      Colmán

16th	*Fintan*
17th	*Aonghus*
18th	*Ronan*
	Hilde
21st	*Colmán*
	Garvan
	Colmán
	Aidan
22nd	*Ultan*
	Maeve
24th	*Bercan*
	Colmán
	Cianán
25th	*Fergal*
27th	*Brendan*
	Cianán
	Fianait
30th	*Cumín*

DECEMBER

1st	*Nessan*
	Brendan
2nd	*Mainchín*
3rd	*Colmán*
4th	*Bercan*
	Mainchín
5th	*Colmán*
	Seanán

6th	*Mellan*
	Nessan
	Beircheart
7th	*Colmán*
8th	*Brendan*
	Finanth
10th	*Colmán*
11th	*Colm*
12th	*Finnian*
	Colmán
13th	*Cormac*
	Brendan
	Colm
14th	*Fintan*
	Ernin
	Colmán
	Cormac
15th	*Flann*
	Cronan
	Colmán
18th	*Caomhán*
	Flannán
	Colmán
	Seanán
	Eimhín
	Cumín
	Ríona

20th	*Dermot*	25th	*Aidan*
	Feidhlimdh	26th	*Jarlath*
	Eoghan		*Laserian*
21st	*Flann*		*Coman*
22nd	*Ultan*	27th	*Fiacha*
	Eimhín		*Colmán*
23rd	*Colmán*	28th	*Killian*
	Ronan		*Fechin*
	Feidhlimidh	29th	*Mainchín*
	Ernin		*Enan*
24th	*Cumín*	31st	*Enda*
	Seanán		
	Maolmhuire		

Gill Books
Hume Avenue, Park West, Dublin 12

www.gillbooks.ie

Gill Books is an imprint of M.H. Gill & Co.

Copyright © Teapot Press Ltd 2008 / 2012
updated edition 2019

ISBN: 978-0-7171-4428-0

This book was created and produced by
Teapot Press Ltd

Printed in Europe

This book is typeset in Garamond and Avenir

A CIP catalogue record for this book is available
from the British Library.

5 4 3

COMPILED AND WRITTEN by Felicity Trotman

EDITED by Lisa Regan, Emily Kearns &
Fiona Biggs

TEXT DESIGNED by Clare Barber

COVER DESIGNED by Alyssa Peacock

PRONUNCIATION GUIDE by
Deirdre Rennison Kunz

Cover photograph: Getty Images